Growth
Hacking

for
dummies®
A Wiley Brand

Growth Hacking

by Anuj Adhiya

Growth Hacking For Dummies®

Published by: **John Wiley & Sons, Inc.,** 111 River Street, Hoboken, NJ 07030-5774, www.wiley.com

Copyright © 2020 by John Wiley & Sons, Inc., Hoboken, New Jersey

Published simultaneously in Canada

For general information on our other products and services, please contact our Customer Care Department within the U.S. at 877-762-2974, outside the U.S. at 317-572-3993, or fax 317-572-4002. For technical support, please visit https://hub.wiley.com/community/support/dummies.

Wiley publishes in a variety of print and electronic formats and by print-on-demand. Some material included with standard print versions of this book may not be included in e-books or in print-on-demand. If this book refers to media such as a CD or DVD that is not included in the version you purchased, you may download this material at http://booksupport.wiley.com. For more information about Wiley products, visit www.wiley.com.

Library of Congress Control Number: 2020904218

ISBN: 978-1-119-61213-1; 978-1-119-61217-9 (ebk); 978-1-119-61216-2 (ebk)

10 9 8 7 6 5 4 3 2 1

Contents at a Glance

Table of Contents

PART 3: APPLYING THE GROWTH HACKING

CHAPTER 6: **Laying the Foundation for Growth**

CHAPTER 7: **Identifying Potential Opportunities
for Growth**

CHAPTER 8: **Prioritizing Your Ideas before You Test Them**

CHAPTER 9: **Testing Ideas and Learning from Them**

Introduction

Welcome to *Growth Hacking For Dummies!*

First, a little bit of history. The concept of growth hacking became popular toward the middle of the 2010's, and its ideas have been used by some of the world's fastest-growing companies to unlock breakout growth. You might already have heard about growth hacking and how it has contributed to the growth of the fastest-growing start-ups over the past decade. You may even have read about how growth hacking has transformed the marketing field as well as how products are developed. What you may still be unclear about is what this growth hacking concept really is.

Growth hacking has always existed, but before the phrase was coined by Sean Ellis, no one had a well-defined way to describe the process — a process, mind you, that was already being practiced with great success in areas of innovation like Silicon Valley. I was lucky enough to find Sean, and then work directly with him, as the popularity of the concept began to explode and helped cement its status as a concept that start-ups cannot ignore if they are to raise the odds of unlocking breakout growth. Start-ups aiming to replicate the success of bigger companies are looking to understand what these successful companies did differently that helped change the trajectory of their growth.

Over the past five years, having been part of (and leading) growth teams and mentoring start-ups on implementing growth hacking methodologies, I found that there was a need to write a digestible guide that someone like me — who previously had no background with start-ups, growth, marketing, or product development — could understand and use.

Growth hacking has now taken its place among other buzzwords among those familiar with the start-up and tech space. In this book, I clear up some of the biggest misunderstandings on what growth hacking is and, most importantly, what it is not. The information in this book will give you the confidence to be successful using the growth hacking methodology. Even if you're familiar with the core concepts of growth hacking, this book may still introduce you to a different way of looking at growth, marketing, and product concepts and may also provide you with some tips on how best to explain to others exactly what growth hacking is.

About This Book

This is a book about clarifying growth hacking's intent. The entire point of the practice is to grow the value you deliver to your customers. You do that by implementing a cross-functional process of testing and learning that involves key stakeholders companywide. This book is as much about the process as it is about the people you call on to execute it and the kind of culture a company needs if this methodology is to take root and bear fruit. This is also a book about how important it is to align your goals with those of your customers and develop empathy for their needs and motivations if you're going to truly find a path to sustainable growth.

When I can, I include real-world examples from my experiences and conversations with other growth professionals.

Whether you're a founder, an executive, or a marketing/growth/product professional, you'll find something worth reading in *Growth Hacking For Dummies*.

Foolish Assumptions

To get the most from this book, I assume that you

>> Have worked for, are working for, or want to be working for a company that is moved beyond product-market fit. You shouldn't be growing something that you haven't validated a need for.

>> Are willing to let data help you make decisions about how you identify your best growth opportunities.

>> Are willing to try something different from what you have done in the past or from what other companies are doing.

>> Are comfortable reading about strategy, process, teams, and data.

>> Have (or will be able to have) access to data or at least want to collect and analyze data.

>> Are looking, of course, for an accessible source that keeps it as simple as possible and provides practical advice about how to get started in the real world, as opposed to what you might find in the content deluge you encounter every day.

Icons Used in This Book

Throughout this book, you'll see these little graphical icons to identify useful paragraphs:

TIP

The Tip icon marks tips and shortcuts that you can take to make a specific task easier.

REMEMBER

The Remember icon marks the information that's especially important to know. To siphon off the most important information in each chapter, just skim these paragraphs.

TECHNICAL STUFF

The Technical Stuff icon marks information of a highly technical nature that you can safely skip over without harm.

WARNING

The Warning icon tells you to watch out! It marks important information that may save you headaches. *Warning:* Don't skip over these warnings!

How This Book Is Organized

The book is arranged into four self-contained parts, each composed of several self-contained chapters. By *self-contained*, I mean that I do my best to tell you everything you need to know about a single topic inside each chapter, other than when I have to reference other parts of the book to connect parts that are legitimately linked.

Here's an overview:

Part 1: Getting Started with Growth Hacking

These early chapters serve as a primer on growth hacking. In this part, you learn to walk before you run, but what you find here lays the foundation for all that comes later. You'll see my definition of growth hacking (and what it is not) and find an introduction to its important concepts, applications, and options. You'll also gain an understanding of the most important skills needed to build a growth team and have it succeed.

Part 2: Seeing Where Growth Opportunities Come From

Many people think of growth hacking as something that is complex or different from what they know. In the beginning of Part 2, you get to see how identifying a customer journey helps you identify potential growth opportunities and lets you see what you can hope to learn from interactions at every step of this journey.

If you read all of Part 2, you'll have examined the different opportunities to provide and enhance value to your customers that you can then double-down on with confidence — versus just going with your gut.

Part 3: Applying the Growth Hacking Process

In this part, I dive deep into the growth hacking methodology. The key ideas you'll walk away with are the importance of a North Star Metric (NSM), building a growth model, and using the growth model to set objectives that you can run tests around. You'll read about how to establish and manage a growth process that allows you to learn rapidly where the biggest signal for growth may be coming from. And though implementing a growth process is a great start, getting companywide adoption of the growth mindset is how you truly lay the foundation for unlocking growth, which you'll also learn how to do.

Part 4: The Part of Tens

If you have ever read another book in the *For Dummies* series, this part of the book is like seeing an old friend again — the friend might be wearing a different outfit, but you will recognize the person right away. The Part of Tens is a collection of interesting growth hacking insights, advice, and warnings broken out into ten easy-to-digest chunks. This part offers ten benefits, ten things to watch for, and the like. These chapters crystalize some concepts you get a chance to read about in the rest of the book, or a way to dig right in to the concepts that matter if you haven't.

Beyond the Book

Although this book broadly covers the growth hacking methodology and process, I can cover only so much in a set number of pages! If you find yourself at the end of this book and thinking, "This was an amazing book — where can I learn more about growth hacking?" check out Chapter 14 or head over to www.dummies.com for more resources.

Cheat Sheet: If you're looking for the traditional *For Dummies* Cheat Sheet, visit www.dummies.com and type **Growth Hacking For Dummies Cheat Sheet** in the Search box.

Growth hacking is a vast domain where you're continually challenged to learn something new, given how fast things change. Unfortunately, one book cannot do justice to all these topics, but, fortunately, that's why you can find more than one book in this world (and people to help write them).

Aside from an introduction to a topic you may not have known much about before, what I aim to do in this book is cover that area of knowledge necessary for a successful application of growth hacking not already covered by other books. I provide a unique (if not sometimes strange) point of view about what *really* matters, honed over many years of practical experiences in the field. What I have to say isn't often what people thought they would find, and I stand by what I think is important enough to share in this format. If you're looking to obtain more depth in a specific technical domain, you can turn to plenty of resources in order to go deeper — not the least of which are other *For Dummies* books.

Other For Dummies Books

You can use a number of related books to drill down into topics I could only briefly touch on in this book — for example, *Data Driven Marketing For Dummies*, by David Semmelroth; *Digital Marketing All-in-One For Dummies*, by Stephanie Diamond; *Marketing For Dummies*, 5th Edition, by Jeanette McMurtry; *Writing Copy For Dummies*, by Jonathan Kranz; *Web Analytics For Dummies*, by Pedro Sostre and Jennifer LeClaire; *SEO For Dummies*, 7th Edition, by Peter Kent; *Advertising For Dummies*, 2nd Edition, by Gary Dahl; *AdWords For Dummies*, by Howie Jacobson, *Affiliate Marketing For Dummies*, by Ted Sudol and Paul Mladjenovic; *Content Marketing For Dummies*, by Susan Gunelius; *Customer Experience For Dummies*, by Roy Barnes and Bob Kelleher; *E-Mail Marketing For Dummies*, 2nd Edition, by John Arnold; *Facebook Marketing All-in-One For Dummies*, 3rd Edition, by Andrea Vahl, John Haydon, and Jan Zimmerman); *Social Media Marketing For Dummies*, 4th Edition, by Shiv Singh and Stephanie Diamond; *Inbound Marketing For Dummies*, by Scott Anderson Miller; *Lead Generation For Dummies*, by Dayna Rothman; *Mobile Marketing For Dummies*, by Michael Becker and John Arnold; *New Product Development For Dummies*, by Robin Karol, Beebe Nelson, and Geoffrey Nicholson); *Public Relations For Dummies*, 2nd Edition, by Eric Yaverbaum, Ilise Benun, Richard Kirshenbaum; and *Selling For Dummies*, 4th Edition, by Tom Hopkins — all published by Wiley. Any and all of these books can produce valuable knowledge, skills, and abilities that can be used to become a more effective growth professional and leader.

Where to Go from Here

You don't need to read this book from cover to cover. You can, if that strategy appeals to you, but it's set up as a reference guide, so you can jump in wherever you need to. Looking for something in particular? Take a peek at the table of contents or index, find the section you need, and then flip to the page to resolve your problem.

1
Getting Started with Growth Hacking

Chapter **1**

Defining Growth Hacking

ooked at one way, this book is years too late, and yet, from lots of other perspectives, this book is right on time. Growth hacking as a concept became highly popular around 2013 and became, for the next few years, the hot new thing everyone was talking about. So, from that perspective, publishing this book in 2020 would appear to be unnecessary because so much discussion on the topic has happened since then and people have already had a chance to learn more about it. The problem I've noticed is that, outside of a relatively small percentage of true practitioners, no one really seemed to articulate the growth hacking concept correctly. Many people applied an interpretation I thought to be unrepresentative of the ethos of the phrase — an ethos I had learned directly from the person who coined *growth hacking* in the first place. And, as with all things that become popular and aren't understood well, people started applying the growth hacking label to things it shouldn't be associated with.

Around 2017, I thought that this would pass because the field was still getting off the ground, but years later I find that there's still a massive lack of clarity when it comes to this topic. This lack of understanding intensifies as you move geographically farther away from centers of innovation like Silicon Valley — and even there, it feels like it isn't understood 100 percent of the time. I have a hypothesis for why that may be the case.

Relatively speaking, the number of people who have actual experience with growth hacking is rather small worldwide. This is simply a function of the high failure rate of start-ups. If you concede that 90 percent of start-ups fail, then simply having the opportunity to grow any start-up is relatively small. This means that the number of people who have had the opportunity to apply the growth hacking methodology successfully is also small.

In my experience, not everyone who's achieved this success ends up wanting to blog about it or talk about it, either at all or with any regularity. I got a sense of this when I worked to recruit growth professionals for the weekly AMA (Ask Me Anything) sessions on GrowthHackers.com. Often, I had on subject matter experts (SMEs) who were not well known or who didn't write and speak as often on the topic.

Unfortunately, such a situation presents an ideal opportunity for those who have not been in environments where growth hacking was practiced as intended to present themselves as "experts" and then offer takes that put forward something that merely approximates growth hacking or, worse, bastardizes the concept to the point where any association with growth hacking starts to have a negative connotation.

This book is my attempt to help people who are just like my former self — in other words, people who have no firsthand experience with growth hacking but finds themselves reading about it all the time. It's also for those who have taken their first steps into the field but don't yet understand it fully because what's out there hasn't been presented in a systematic, easy-to-understand way.

Defining Growth Hacking Goals

In relative terms, growth hacking as a concept is quite new. Sean Ellis coined it in 2010 in his seminal "Find a Growth Hacker for Your Start-up" blog post. (See Figure 1-1.) The concept gained popularity mostly among Silicon Valley practitioners until early 2012, when Andrew Chen wrote his "Growth Hacker is the new VP of Marketing" post (https://andrewchen.co/how-to-be-a-growth-hacker-an-airbnbcraigslist-case-study), when the phrase truly entered mainstream consciousness.

This is not to say that growth hacking was not a thing before Sean coined the phrase. It's just that no one had come up with a way to describe it well.

FIGURE 1-1:
The blog post that started it all.

Sean defined a *growth hacker* as "a person whose true north is growth. Everything they do is scrutinized by its potential impact on scalable growth." After your company has found product-market fit (a measure of the degree to which a product satisfies a strong market demand), you need to find a way to grow quickly. (I'll talk about product-market fit more in the next section.) The explicit role of the person who would spearhead these growth efforts would be to, as Sean also talks about in this post, "[find] scalable, repeatable and sustainable ways to grow the business." Some concepts were implicit in the words he used in this last statement that have been clarified in various contexts over time but are worth summarizing here:

» **Growth had to be sustainable.** You cannot build a sustainable business if it's one that doesn't continue to deliver value over time. Unfortunately, we don't live in a world where people give us money for nothing on an ongoing basis. So, we must provide value. And, given that this is a business and all businesses must grow, it follows that the value we deliver must also grow over time.

» **Sustainability is a function of scalable and repeatable activities.** When something is repeatable, it's a process. When an activity or a process is scalable, it means that it can adapt to larger demands — whether that's more users or some other business need — leading to greater stability and competitiveness, which in turn helps growth be sustainable. This also tells us that it will never be just one thing that does the trick — it will always be a combination of many elements working together, each playing its part and leading the way to explosive growth.

> **>> These scalable and repeatable ways to build a sustainable business would have to be *found*.** By definition, there are no silver bullets. Every business is different. Every context and every audience has its own variables. What works in one instance isn't guaranteed to work in another. You will have to put in the hard work of seeing what works (and doesn't work) for you. The only way to find what works is to just try things out and see what happens. It also follows that, to see what works, those things must be testable and measurable to understand their impact. The more things you try and the faster you try them, the quicker you'll learn about what truly delivers value to your customers.

REMEMBER

It's never a situation where you're just trying things randomly. You take advantage of what you already know about your customers to inform hypotheses about what might work across the entire customer journey.

To bring this back down to earth, the goal of growth hacking is to be *continually and rapidly testing, across the customer journey, to learn about activities that can be systemized as processes to grow the value that a business provides its customers.* It is as simple and as complicated as that. Any definition that doesn't at least cover all these key aspects is talking about something else — not growth hacking.

This book is dedicated to giving you a framework for thinking about how to find these scalable, repeatable, and sustainable ways to grow your business.

Working through the Basics

Before you think about growing anything, you must have a product that is growable. In other words, you must have validated the need for your product first (popularly known as *product-market fit*). You have no business (literally and figuratively) growing something that you have not confirmed, through testing and learning, that it's something people want.

TIP

Sean Ellis has created a survey to help you qualitatively ascertain how close to product-market fit you might be. You can find it at `https://pmfsurvey.com`.

Even before you get to product-market fit, you must know — or at least have a hypothesis for — the value your product provides. This starting point for all growth hacking activities serves as the first part of the growth hacking process. Figure 1-2 shows the process in graphic form, but it can be summarized as follows:

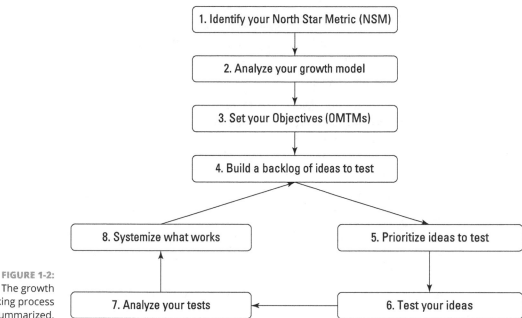

FIGURE 1-2:
The growth
hacking process
summarized.

1. **Identify your North Star Metric (NSM).**

The NSM is the number that quantifies the value your product provides to your users or customers. Every product will have its own NSM because every product provides value differently. (Google provides value through search results, for example, whereas Lyft provides value with rides on demand.) When I've asked people what number quantifies the value their product delivers to their users, it generally is the first time they've been asked that question. I then get silence followed mostly by their statement that their NSM is revenue or money — and they're mostly wrong when they say that.

Chapter 6 goes into more detail on this topic, along with examples.

2. **Analyze your growth model.**

If every product provides value differently, then the way to grow every product also cannot be the same. Too many different variables are at play. So, you have to understand what the customer journey looks like to be able to identify all the points within it that contribute to growth. (The *customer journey,* put simply, is the collection of interactions between your company and a customer over the duration of your relationship. For more on the customer journey, see Chapter 5.) This analysis is based on quantitative and qualitative data to help you understand key points within the customer journey that represent the biggest opportunity you could exploit or the problem that, if you were to tackle it, could potentially lead to greater growth.

Chapter 6 talks a lot more about how to go about this because this step is critical to focusing your team on activities that have the highest potential to impact your NSM.

3. **Set objectives.**

   After you know what part of the customer journey you'll focus on, set an objective on which to focus tests. Set a time frame of 30 to 90 days in which to test so that you can better understand the impact of your tests on your NSM. If NSMs are your long-term goal, then your objectives are your short-term goals. The quantification of any objective becomes your One Metric That Matters (OMTM).

   In Chapter 7, I talk more about how and why setting objectives helps the team test only around an area of maximum potential impact.

4. **Build a backlog of ideas to test.**

   After you know what your objectives are, you need to come up with ideas — hypotheses, really — to test. Hopefully, coming up with new ideas is an ongoing process on your team, but every new objective presents opportunities to think anew about what options might be tried. Everybody on the team (and in the broader company) should be encouraged to contribute ideas to test. Chapter 7 has more detail on how to come up with testable ideas.

5. **Prioritize ideas to test.**

   After you have a list of things you can try, you need to identify which ones might have the greatest potential. You can use any number of prioritization frameworks that will help you pick the ideas with the best potential. (See Chapter 8 for more on prioritization frameworks.)

6. **Test your ideas.**

   More than anything else, growth hacking is about learning quickly what works and doesn't work. So, when you test ideas, you perform a minimum viable test to learn whether it's worth your while to continue testing in that area. This means constructing your test correctly with respect to any design, copy, engineering, and measurement specifications as appropriate and then launching the test effectively.

   REMEMBER

   To learn faster, you also need to test faster. Build a cadence of multiple tests a week (or biweekly) so that you can be extremely agile about spotting opportunities. (Chapter 9 guides you through this process.)

7. **Analyze your tests.**

   Tests that you don't learn from are useless. As soon as you have enough data, analyze your tests to glean any insights those tests may have provided. All the time you're trying to understand why a test worked or didn't work? What can you take away from the learnings that you can apply to the next set of tests, irrespective of whether the answer is to double down on something that seems to work or move in a different direction? The second half of Chapter 9 guides you through how to learn from your tests.

8. **Systemize what works.**

   To capitalize on tests that have worked, you need to make them part of how you operate moving forward. Depending on the kind of test, you can do this in one of two ways: Make the change you tested part of your product by coordinating with the product development team or, if the test was a result of multiple steps (like generating content), create a process that represents a playbook that anyone can repeat in order to achieve similar results.

Since growth never ends, growth hacking is a continual process. As you continue testing against an objective and understand more about whether you've extracted the most gain from that opportunity, you'll make decisions on whether to continue testing where you have been or to evaluate your growth model for new areas of opportunity and repeat the process over again.

REMEMBER

The greatest growth hack you'll find is building a culture of testing and learning. Creating such a culture is incredibly hard, but if you can pull it off, you'll have put yourself in a position to provide even greater value to your customers than your competition can.

Recognizing the Distinctive Nature of Growth Hacking

Given that many other popular product development and marketing methodologies are out there (all whose ultimate purpose is to grow a business), it's useful to understand how and where they differ from growth hacking proper.

Traditional marketing versus growth hacking

Traditional marketing has always been about getting customers to (become interested in) your product. Its major focus is on promoting finished products, and its biggest goal is to fill your sales pipeline and generate revenue. It does this through a variety of methods — content marketing, search engine optimization, public relations, social media ads, and anything else that will bring attention and interest to the product they're selling.

Morgan Brown, coauthor with Sean Ellis of the book *Hacking Growth: How Today's Fastest-Growing Companies Drive Breakout Success* (Random House), describes growth hacking as "experiment driven marketing focused primarily on how the product is used to create growth both from the distribution and retention side. The key differentiator being the product-level focus vs. the channel-level focus of traditional marketing effort."

Did you catch that difference? Growth hacking relies more on the product itself to unlock growth instead of simply attracting people to the product. Whereas traditional marketers may no doubt be optimizing for how they draw people to the product, growth professionals consider the entire customer journey, with an explicit focus on retention. Because of this product-level focus, growth professionals can team up with product-and-engineering folks to learn more about what it will take to get someone to not only come to the product but then also remain a devoted customer because they experience so much value from the product.

So, it should be clear that although traditional marketing and growth hacking have some overlap — so much so that practitioners on both sides of the aisle may even use many of the same techniques — they have fundamentally different goals.

Lean start-up versus growth hacking

A 1-line definition from the Lean Start-up site, co-founded by Eric Ries, says that Lean Start-up provides a) a scientific approach to creating and managing start-ups and b) a proven way to get a desired product to customers' hands faster. Some of this sounds just like growth hacking, doesn't it?

Now, we were lucky at GrowthHackers early on to have an AMA (Ask Me Anything) session that featured both Eric Ries (the author of the most famous book on the lean start-up methodology) and Sean Ellis. To no one's surprise, folks were eager to find out whether the two approaches were substantially different.

Eric said that the lean start-up approach emphasized two coequal parts of any start-up or business strategy: the value hypothesis and the growth hypothesis, with both given equal importance. However, in terms of what's written about the lean start-up methodology, more attention has been paid to value hypothesis activities. Even Sean admits that, until that particular AMA, he had thought of lean start-up as being about making something growable (validating product-market fit, in other words) and growth hacking as the process of growing it.

Morgan Brown noted in that same AMA session that, whereas growth is definitely part of the lean start-up approach, the growth hypothesis has elements that might have been ignored because of the product-centric thinking of Silicon Valley — a thinking that, in the past, had espoused a "build it and they will come" mentality. He further hypothesized that the perception that the growth aspect was somehow missing from the lean start-up approach could have lit the spark for the growth hacking movement.

But getting back to how Sean Ellis articulated the differences between a lean start-up approach and growth hacking, the one thing Ellis felt was 100 percent true about growth hacking is that you shouldn't even be thinking about growing a product that has not been validated yet. All you'd do is expose potential users and customers to a product they'll come to hate, ensuring that they'll never want to return to it in the future.

REMEMBER

Don't let all this talk about terminology become the start of some semantic discussion about whether one methodology is better than the other. What you should be doing instead is taking concepts that work for you from wherever you get them so that you can get the results you want. Nothing is more important than that.

Agile product development versus growth hacking

The most consequential differences between agile product development and growth hacking are their goals and rhythms. Agile product development's primary focus is to develop a product that works. Growth hacking is about developing a product that attracts and retains customers. You could say that product retention, monetizing users, and making the product experience so great that it drives word of mouth are the product team's responsibility. The growth team would constantly evaluate all these aspects in order to figure out the best way to get users to the product and provide them with a great first experience. Again, you can see a bit of an overlap here. Both focus heavily on the user and delivering something of value, but the way they do it is quite different.

The other difference between the two is that agile processes like Scrum create sprint backlogs that define the tasks for the next two, three, or four weeks. A growth hacking process, on the other hand, is based on a high tempo of experimentation with weekly or biweekly sprints that can show wins in the most unpredictable places and times and that could be systemized within the product experience. This makes it nearly impossible to align the growth process with product development sprints.

REMEMBER

There are other alignment challenges as well in lining up testing with product development that I cover later in this book, but the tension between prioritizing changes based on tests versus new features development or bug-fixing is real.

PRODUCT-LED GROWTH VERSUS GROWTH HACKING

The phrase *product-led growth,* coined by the venture capital firm OpenView Venture Partners, has started to become more fashionable of late. There's even a book on the market by Wes Bush as well as communities starting to sprout around this notion. It's been used to help define how companies have built their growth strategies around their products. Though the term may be new, again, people have been using product-led growth strategies for a while.

I asked Wes Bush to clarify the distinction for me during an AMA session on GrowthHackers. He noted that growth hacking is an iterative process that you can use to grow *any* type of business. He also observed that not every business can be product led. This is especially true of complex products that require demos and multiple meetings to convince someone of the value of the product. Finalizing the sale can take days or weeks. This model of operating is common for traditional sales-led companies. Product-led growth, on the other hand, is specific to a subset of businesses, where the "time-to-value" is really fast and is a function of someone being able to use the product without jumping through any hoops. This in turn allows people to start experiencing the value of the product much faster.

There are other criteria that apply specifically to product-led companies but for now the distinction that I hold in my head is that product-led growth applies to a subset of the products that you could apply the growth hacking methodology to. Again, this is not intended to stir a debate on which methodology is better as much as having an understanding as to what differentiates them.

Steering Clear of Growth Hacking Obstacles

As with any idea that's hasn't found a universal understanding yet, people are bound to voice their — at times, rather unfounded —opinions about it. Given that I learned about growth hacking from the guy who coined the phrase, I've had the opportunity to understand better than most what it truly is and is not about. In this section, I address some of the more problematic "hot takes" that folks have come up with when it comes to this topic.

The phrase itself

I think it's fair to say that there is a fair amount of hatred for the term *growth hacking*. Sean Ellis has said on multiple occasions that he intended for the term to be controversial. After all, it's hard to imagine anything worse than coining a new phrase and then having people ignore it. The fact that people have a strong reaction to the term *growth hacking* gives it the attention it needs in order to allow practitioners to show others the way. So, if you're one of those who has a visceral reaction to it, know that, by doing so, you've let yourself through the very door that Sean Ellis intended for you to step through in order to learn more about it. This is nothing short of marketing genius.

Getting caught up in the "hacking" part

Let's face it: Many people equate growth hacking with spammy tactics, shortcuts, tricks, and ploys. You'll see this regularly when people come across an under-handed tactic and derisively cry out a version of, "Ugh, stop with the growth hacking."

You can see why this might be the case because, when people think of hacking, they think of the typical Hollywood stereotype of someone doing something illegal. It hasn't helped that people indulging in terrible tactics have co-opted the phrase as a badge of honor, making those who are victims of spammy tactics feel like this is what growth hackers do.

This is unfortunate because what Sean Ellis intended for the "hacking" part of the phrase to speak to is the creativity, subject matter expertise, and sheer dogged-ness needed to endure failure as you seek out avenues of breakout growth.

Thinking that growth has to come at the cost of the customer experience

This heading, which is related to associating growth hacking with the spammy tactics I mention earlier, implies that the business cares only about itself and that the customer's only role is to hand over money or data that can be used by the business to make more money. Again, because the phrase has been co-opted by some bad actors, it comes across as if all growth hackers indulge in such practices, when nothing could be further from the truth.

If anything, sustainable growth only comes from a deep understanding of your customers' motivations and how you use that understanding to grow the value provided to them. It's just not logical to think that you can grow value if you do these one-time tricks, which by definition are unsustainable.

Thinking that it's about quick hits and tactics

If you search online for the term *growth hacking,* you'll find hundreds of articles on how someone growth-hacked something or compiled a top-ten list of growth hacks that every start-up must complete and a ton of other variations, all of which focus on tactics. The way these are written seems to imply that if you simply replicated what they did, you'd find the same kind of success, when nothing could be further from the truth. Everyone's context is different. The number of variables in play are innumerable.

Growth hacking is not and has never been about tactics. It's always been about a process and taking advantage of product- and system-level growth opportunities. It's always been about rigorous testing to improve how the product drives distribution and retention.

Thinking that there's a magical growth hacker

I talk more about characteristics of a growth hacker in Chapter 2, but it's important to know that there is no single magical growth hacker that will make miracles happen. Even if Sean Ellis were to join a new company tomorrow, there's no way he could guarantee any level of success, let alone anything as big as what he's done in his earlier roles at Dropbox, Eventbrite, LogMeIn, and Lookout. All he could realistically promise is the ability to learn about what works and what doesn't by testing quickly and building a culture of testing.

Anyone providing any guarantee that they will be able to "growth-hack your business" is flat-out lying. If anything, growth is about cross-functional teams that include marketing, engineering, and product development working together to unlock new ways for products to grow.

Thinking that only the growth team is responsible for growth

Nothing could be further from the truth. Now, is the growth team primarily responsible for driving activities that lead to growth? Of course! But to think that you can just create a growth team and they'll get the job done on their own is a fallacy. As you'll consistently read in the book, growth is a cross-functional process. Everybody in the company has to be on board with what the growth team is doing and has a supporting role to play. Some of these roles are closer to the growth team and have more frequent interactions. Others, less so. But everyone has to play because growth is a team sport.

Thinking that you need a background in product development or marketing

From firsthand experience, I can say that thinking you need a background in product development or marketing is complete nonsense. Before I joined Growth-Hackers, I had no experience with marketing, product development, growth, or anything start-up related by way of formal education or on-the-job experience. I have degrees in chemistry and biochemistry, yet here you are, reading a book on growth hacking written by me.

Growth hacking is simply about applying the scientific method to marketing and product development. If you ever ran an experiment in science lab when you were in school, you already understand the methodology. Now it's simply about applying it to a different context. This is easier to do than I realized when I started running tests at GrowthHackers. If you're able to do your research, follow the process, and let the data guide you, you'll be ahead of most people trying to figure out their next step.

Thinking that you need to be a coder

Don't get me wrong: Coding skills help. But they are not absolutely necessary. Many of the biggest names in growth do not know how to code (much). This misconception also stems a bit from the hacking part of the phrase. If anything, the implication is that you should be as scrappy as a coder might be or that you should, as a coder would, think through different ways to solve for a solution.

Thinking that growth comes from acquisition

GrowthHackers.com has a job board and I could regularly see postings for a growth hacker. (More on "growth hacker" as a job title is later in this list.) On reading the job descriptions, it wasn't uncommon to see that what they really wanted was a marketer — someone proficient in a specific acquisition channel, in other words.

When I was deciding on my role after GrowthHackers, I saw innumerable job listings with the same misconception played out over and over again. People really wanted a person who could drive traffic to their site or app but because people don't understand the concept well enough, you get this thinking that growth is a function of acquisition. Not to mention "growth hacker" (or "growth marketer") is trendier to say than marketer.

Thinking that the "famous growth hacks" did all the hard work

When I first wrote the outline of this chapter, I thought I'd reiterate some of the topics that have become the stuff of legend in the growth hacking world. These are topics that have been written about quite a bit, such as Dropbox's referral mechanism, Hotmail's PS line that had a free link back to its site to get a free account, or Airbnb taking professional photos of the hosts' homes and others that led to breakout growth for these companies. These are all just a Google search away.

Though these individual tasks certainly led to big wins for these companies, writing about them again simply perpetuates the myth that you need just one home run and everything else will take care of itself. Whenever these topics are written about, rarely is there any mention of the tests that came before that led to insights that laid the foundation for these big wins to manifest themselves. Similarly, nothing is ever mentioned about all the tests that came afterward to optimize these big wins and to find other opportunities for growth, even if they were nothing like the most famous win.

Are these famous, big wins inspirational? For sure. But, as I've said, to take them at face value and think that if you just did the same thing, you'd get the same results is foolish. If anything, the lesson from reading about how any company grew is to understand what their process was of learning more about their customers' motivations and how they found their way to meet those needs to unlock growth.

Thinking that you can just call yourself a growth hacker

If you do a search on LinkedIn, as of this writing you'll find over 25,000 people with "growth hacker" in their job title. It's funny in two ways. First, the guy that came up with growth hacking has never used it as a job title. Look all you want. You won't find it anywhere. Secondly, it's not a job title! Growth hacking is something you do and in many ways this rampant (mis)use within job titles perfectly encapsulates the pervasive misconceptions around what growth hacking truly is.

Morgan Brown said it best when he opined in one of the discussions in the Growth-Hackers community that growth hacking is an "ex post facto" title. In other words, you only earn it once you've actually done the hard work of driving growth. You don't earn it by adding it to your LinkedIn profile.

WHAT'S IN A NAME?

It is no secret that many people detest the term *growth hacking*. I'll confess that I'm not a raving fan of the phrase myself, but neither do I mind it. The dislike comes mainly from three sources — people who

- Believe that the phrase is just corny or overly pretentious
- Believe that it's a buzzword that really doesn't represent anything new
- Get caught up in the *hacking* part of the phrase

Whatever it may be, there's no hard-and-fast rule that growth hacking needs to be called growth hacking. I've never heard Sean Ellis ever say this, either. Even throughout this book, I use *growth* and *growth hacking* interchangeably. I've also seen it called *growth marketing* or *agile marketing*. Even with these descriptors, you'll find people making passionate arguments about how big the distinction is when you choose different words.

In my view, it's all academic. Call it what you want. Use whatever phrase will make you feel less embarrassed to be associated with it in public. No one will be offended if you choose to define it in a way that makes more sense to you.

As I repeat throughout this book, growth hacking is a process. The sole goal of this process is to test and learn more about how to grow the value you deliver to your users so that you can build a sustainable business. If that means you need to add definitions, criteria, or caveats to make it more understandable and actionable, you should do that. If you believe that it's just your normal product development process, that's what it is. Growth hacking as an idea is big enough to incorporate all that in the service of adding value to the customer.

A great analogy is the martial art Jeet Kune Do, developed by Bruce Lee. The martial art itself was a mashup of various techniques that Bruce Lee found useful. The primary techniques, indeed, were ones that were most useful to him based on his preferred fighting style. But the entire absorb-what-is-useful ethos was central to Jeet Kune Do's philosophy. All of what worked for Bruce Lee did not work for every one of his students. And though they all had to learn some basics, when it came to developing true expertise with the art, they all had to apply these fundamental principles to their individual contexts and preferences to be able to become proficient at Jeet Kune Do. Growth hacking is just like that to me.

In my mind, the place where you need to take a stand is to insist that growth hacking is not a series of spammy tactics designed to trick people and make money while they're still confused about what just happened. If you buy into the central tenets of growth

(continued)

(continued)

hacking as I've presented them, you've just drafted yourself into the growing worldwide army of those who defend the principles of growth hacking as they were intended to be.

This means actively chiming in when you see or hear conversations where people deride a tactic as "growth hacking" (by literally using the quote marks), when it clearly isn't representative of the intent of the practice. There are far more bad actors out there than those who care about doing the hard work of building sustainable businesses by tirelessly working to help customers achieve their goals. At the same time, not enough of us are standing up for growth hacking's core principles. One of my hopes is that, by reading this book, you'll have the ammunition to do just that. Idealistic as it may sound, together, one day soon, we'll be able to beat back the tide of misinformation and misunderstanding around this topic and just do the job of serving our users and customers better every day.

Chapter **2**

Building Growth Hacking Skills

G rowth hacking is all about aligning your entire company around a process that grows value for its customers. You're correct to assume that *that* won't happen on its own, but you may not have a clear idea of *how* exactly it will happen.

Your starting point is the person who will be responsible for leading your company's growth efforts. The *growth lead,* irrespective of the official title, is the person normally associated with the growth hacker label, but that's not entirely accurate. (This chapter, as well as Chapter 3, goes into more detail about it.) If you're on the core team that's been tasked with growth, by definition you're a growth hacker as well, at least in my view, but for the sake of simplicity, I'll use *growth lead* as the stand-in for the *growth hacker* label.

Determining the Growth Hacker's Skill Set

The basic growth process for any company follows the same pattern:

1. Identify your North Star Metric (NSM).

2. Analyze your growth model.

3. Set objectives.

4. Build a pool of ideas to test.

5. Prioritize ideas to test.

6. Test ideas.

7. Analyze your tests.

8. Systematize what works.

Assume that, as a business, you've already identified your NSM. (For more on the North Star Metric, see Chapter 1.) It follows, then, that whoever will lead growth understands and agrees with it. (So Step 1 is taken care of.) The person's first critical job is to understand and build out a model for your product to grow. (That's Step 2.) This doesn't have to be a complicated model, but it should contain the key growth levers and be able to show how pulling those levers will help your company grow.

After they've identified a growth model, the next key function in this role is to choose which part of the growth model the company should focus on. (This is Step 3, setting objectives.)

TIP

Given that much of the growth model in many cases encompasses the actual product experience in many cases, the growth lead tends to be a product person. This makes sense, because making the product experience itself more valuable is tightly correlated to understanding user motivations.

What isn't obvious here is that, along with the focus on whatever part of the growth model is being prioritized, there will also always be the need to test (and scale) new customer acquisition channels. (I talk about this topic more in Chapter 5.) No channel retains its efficiency forever, however. Growth leads are always looking ahead to find the next best channel, so as to not get caught flat-footed and stall growth.

All other steps in the growth process focus on building a testing program. So the third key job entails not only the regular work of managing the testing process but also engaging cross-functional teams to participate in the program and creating a culture of learning companywide, if it is to be truly successful. (For more on testing, see the chapters in Part 3.) It's helpful if you have had some project (or product) management experience as the process is much the same with managing scope, resources, and time as part of your regular sprints. If you've never done this before, Part 3 will provide you with a foundation for how to manage the process.

All these skills need to be learned, and there is no question that it takes hard work to develop mastery across the spread of knowledge you'd need to acquire in order to become truly proficient at growth.

REMEMBER

You should not be hiring for growth until you have achieved product-market fit. (I mention this point at various places in this book.) After your product has had some organic growth as a function of achieving product-market fit, hire your first growth person to take a systematic approach designed to build on that natural growth.

Inspecting the Growth Hacker's Toolbox

A popular construct for the varied skill set a growth-hacker-type person should possess is that of the *T-shaped marketer.* (See Figure 2-1.) The use of the word *marketer* here has always been a bit confusing to me, given that traditional marketing has been focused more on increasing brand awareness and acquiring leads versus the focus on the full customer lifecycle that defines any true growth professional. Putting that aside, however, the construct itself is useful in demonstrating the depth and breadth of knowledge needed to have the ability to continually grow value for your users and, as a result, for your product. Being T-shaped means having general knowledge of many skills and having deep knowledge or ability in one or a few areas.

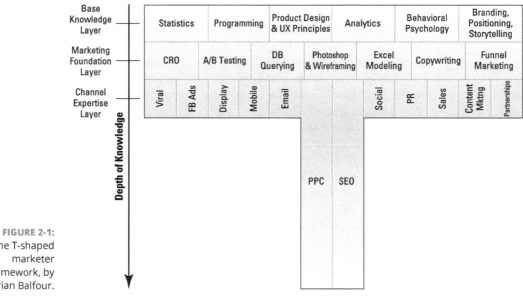

FIGURE 2-1:
The T-shaped marketer framework, by Brian Balfour.

The first version of this T-shaped marketer construct that I noticed was the one created by Brian Balfour in 2013. The idea here was that you could develop a T-shaped approach to acquiring the skills necessary to do your job: In other words, you could develop broad knowledge of the basics, key processes, and activities of a growth program and then build deep expertise within specific channels.

The *T* would have three layers, starting from the top:

>> **Base Knowledge:** Consists of those non-growth, more generalized topics that nevertheless have an impact across multiple aspects of the growth program

>> **Marketing Foundation:** Much like the base knowledge layer, consists of marketing and growth fundamentals that inform all activities at one point or another

>> **Channel Expertise:** Knowing how to work with the channels that are performing well today and finding those that could work well tomorrow

It's no surprise that these layers of the *T* correspond well to the three key jobs of a growth lead: Understand how products grow (necessitating a broad understanding of your product and the value it provides), focus on where the best growth opportunity for your product lies (requiring more specific growth/marketing skills), and test new channels (yep — calling for channel expertise).

Since Balfour released this concept (which itself was inspired by an earlier, more SEO-specific version of the same idea, by Mike Tekula), others have expanded on what specific skills are part of the *T* as an understanding of growth and marketing has evolved and as new channels have emerged. Some of these updates have even repositioned whether certain skills might lie within the base layer or the Marketing Foundation layer.

To a certain extent, I believe that the debate might be academic. What is clear, though, is that as our understanding of growth hacking has evolved and as the inevitable expectations of growth professionals have increased, what may be considered a part of any specific layer has evolved as well.

TIP

Even though everything you've been reading in this chapter has been from the lens of the growth lead, it should be apparent that the *T* for a growth lead would look quite different from the *T* of, say a data analyst, community manager, or content marketer on the team, because they have different strengths that they need to go deep on. This may mean that, for some people, the stem of the *T* — that part that represents specific channel expertise — may not necessarily show up in the middle. For others — those who go deeper in multiple channels, for example — their *T* may end up looking more like an *M* — 3 "legs" rather than 1. Take the *T* framework for what it is — a starting point to understand where you could make choices on where to go deep.

Writing about each of these growth skills in depth would merit its own book, but knowing in general terms the universe of skills waiting to be tapped is beneficial because it gives you a starting point for where to attack based on the knowledge you may already have or on personal preferences. Having this general overview, then, will help you to think about building the next set of skills from that point on. Based on the original Balfour framework, my personal experience, conversations with other growth professionals, and iterations since, these skills turn out to be similar to this list (in no particular order):

>> **Base Knowledge Layer**

- *Behavioral psychology:* A theme I return to just because it's so important is that growth is about growing value for your customers. That means having an understanding of why they do what they do (and don't do). To understand their pain points and the goals they want to achieve, you simply have to have a knowledge of behavioral psychology. You could think of this area as an extension of the process of research for customer development as a way to understand your ideal customer better. I don't think it's a stretch to say that if you understand behavioral psychology, your ability to grow almost any product or service effectively increases dramatically.

- *Branding/positioning/storytelling:* Part of understanding your customers is also identifying the particular value of your product or service and communicating it in a way that resonates with them. The cliché is true: "If you build it for everyone, you build it for no one." Here's how you learn about how your offering is different from your competitors in order to craft narratives that stand out from the crowd. This is hard to do because this set of skills is all about creating excitement around your *company* — in other words, it goes beyond excitement about the product itself. It's the sum of the experience people have while interacting with your company along its many touch points. And because it's not just one thing, it's a difficult skill to master.

- *Customer journey mapping:* This area overlaps in many ways with building a growth model, but it's generally more detailed as you understand all the different ways people can experience your product and all the touch points involved, depending on where they came from and where they landed and all the combinations therein that ultimately lead them to value. Part of knowing how to do mapping correctly involves seeing how painful it can sometimes be for customers as they make their way along their journey; it's a great way to build empathy for your customers by designing better ways for them to reach their goals.

- *Design/user experience design:* As you start to understand the customer journey, you need to start putting that understanding into practice in the form of wireframes for subjects like onboarding flows, checkout flows, or even detailing how new features work. You obviously won't turn into a design specialist, but you need to understand how aspects of design impact product, marketing, and growth as a whole. As you do more of this, you'll start to develop the "good taste" necessary for understanding what great design and a great user experience look and feel like.

- *Statistics fundamentals:* Face it. You have to deal with numbers — a lot. When doing testing, it's helpful to have a basic understanding of concepts like statistical significance, confidence intervals, p-tests, and sample sizes. And whether you know it already or not, you'll create lots of spreadsheets where you track all sorts of numbers and goals.

- *Basic HTML and CSS:* You can find plenty of drag-and-drop templates to work with for all sorts of web design tools that you're sure to use regularly. But soon you'll realize that whenever you want to customize just a little, you'll be pointed to the dreaded Advanced mode, which requires you to know at least some HTML or CSS. Having even basic familiarity here makes you more independent, whether it's the layout of your email, landing pages, or even your blog.

❯❯ Marketing Foundation Layer

- *Data and Analytics:* Growth is nothing if not informed by data. Every tool you use will generate data, and you'll have the task of stitching together all these pieces of data into a unified picture. So, understanding data analytics and how to integrate them is vital. Data is a true rabbit hole, so before you get sucked into all it can offer, you should know what data can and cannot show you and what good data analysis looks like. Only when you know what is happening and marry that with an understanding of why it's happening can you optimize effectively. If you can learn to be consistent with what and how you measure data, the better positioned you'll be in order to understand how to move key numbers in the right direction.

  As you gain more experience here, you'll find that you'll want to slice your data in ways that just aren't possible by using standard analytics tools. Having some basic SQL querying knowledge can help you get the data in the right format from your database. And even after that, you'll likely want to manipulate the data in a spreadsheet to extract even more insights, so knowing what's possible within Excel or comparable programs is useful as well.

- *Conversion rate optimization (CRO):* The CRO process and the tactics used will help you uncover the biggest obstacles in the way of your product's growth and/or the largest opportunities to unlock that growth. Doing this results in more conversions or more people doing what you wanted them to do, be it signing up for your product or making more sales. This plays into every test you run across the customer journey, whether it's within your product or with any acquisition channel.

- *Funnel marketing:* This area takes your knowledge of the customer journey to the next step, where you can start to get a deeper understanding of how and why people move through each stage of the journey. Here you'll try to dig deeper into what it is exactly that tips someone over to becoming a customer or what keeps them coming back; as always, your goal is to continually improve the customer experience and the value you provide.

- *Copywriting:* Understanding your current customer's psychology (as well as the psychology of potential customers) should inform everything you use to communicate about your product. This manifests itself in everything from ad copy to site copy and any content you generate within any channel.

REMEMBER

You don't necessarily have to be an amazing copywriter if you have writers on your team, but you should be able to communicate messaging strategies to the writers if that's the case.

- *Testing and experiment design:* Testing is an aspect of CRO, but it involves more than just running tests. This also goes to developing a growth mindset that is all about gaining insights. And, when you run tests, you need to design them properly so that you can extract the greatest level of learning, and the right kind of learning, from them. (Much of Part 3 in this book focuses precisely on this topic.)

- *Pricing:* It's not uncommon to see pricing be a function of guesswork or simply following what someone else is doing. But, as with all other aspects of your business, this too requires a deliberate approach that's a combination of qualitative and quantitative data. Decisions you make here, unsurprisingly, have a direct impact on your ability to survive and grow.

- *Automation:* As you start using more tools, you'll quickly realize that managing them becomes a hassle. Coordinating data and interactions between them becomes critical, and doing it manually quickly stops being an option. Knowing how to automate these connections and interactions using purpose-built tools or application programming interfaces (APIs) will become a key advantage, because you'll be able to make your entire system work more efficiently by automating repetitive, critical, and time-sensitive tasks like data transfers, data syncing, and reporting.

- *Collaboration:* As you and your team start running more tests, you'll inevitably need assistance and involvement from other groups. Learning how to influence and bridge competing needs is invaluable, in not only keeping your testing program going but also spreading adoption companywide.

>> Channel Expertise Layer

- *Viral marketing:* You grow by encouraging your users to refer other users.

- *Public relations (PR):* Your name is mentioned in traditional media outlets, like newspapers, magazines, and TV.

- *Unconventional PR:* Do something unexpected, like initiate publicity stunts or do business in a way that no one else does, in order to draw media attention.

- *Search engine marketing (SEM):* Show targeted ads to consumers who are already searching online in order to solve a particular problem.

- *Social and display ads:* Run ads on popular sites like YouTube or Facebook to reach new customers.

- *Offline ads:* Run ads on TV, radio, or billboards; in newspapers or magazines; or create flyers and other local advertisements.

- *Search engine optimization:* Ensure that your website shows up for key search results so that you can cheaply acquire lots of highly targeted traffic.

- *Content marketing:* Generate high-quality content that attracts an outsized level of attention from people interested in a topic, which in turn drives traffic to the business.

- *Email marketing:* After you have a prospect's attention, use email to convert, retain, and monetize them.

- *Engineering as marketing:* Build tools, calculators, or widgets that people can use for free, and in turn they give you their contact information so that you can nurture them into customers.

- *Targeting blogs:* Target niche blogs (or *microinfluencers*) to talk about your product to their highly engaged audiences.

- *Partnerships:* Partner up and create strategic relationships that produce a mutual benefit.

- *Sales:* Create sustainable and scalable processes to make it easier for customers to buy. This is mostly seen in the B2B world, where transactions can be complex.

- *Affiliate programs:* Enhance your distribution by allowing other people or companies to sell your product for a commission.

- *Existing platforms:* Piggyback on a huge platform like Facebook or an app store so that you leverage the attention of their large user base toward your product.

- *Trade shows:* Showcase your product to a specific industry and, more importantly, to decision-makers who attend such events.

- *Offline events:* Sponsor or host offline events — of any size — putting your product in front of a qualified audience in order to generate interest.

- *Speaking engagements:* Speak at high-profile events, which results in your product being promoted to an interested audience as a natural consequence of promoting you.

- *Community building:* Grow by forming passionate communities around your product.

TIP

Given the number of channels out there, a question you may have is, "Which one(s) should I specialize in?" One way to do this is to start with channels for which you have a natural interest or aptitude. It's just easier to stay motivated that way. If you then layer on what the needs of your business might be, that gives you another lens to further narrow your focus to a channel that might be a win-win for everyone. Start with one, but if you have the ability, try to develop expertise in two channels. That way, you can get a leg up on the competition, because most folks stick to a single channel. (For more on channels, see Chapter 3.)

Here's another suggestion I hear a lot: If you have the flexibility to do so, focus on a new or emerging channel. In doing so, you become one of the first people to learn about the dynamics of that channel, which (if it becomes popular) you've become an "expert" in. And, because everyone else is rushing to catch up to where you are, there won't be many people like you, further burnishing your brand as well as personal opportunities to leverage what you've learned.

If you don't have the flexibility to pick emerging channels, consider whether you can specialize in a couple of channels that people generally don't do together. For example, people who are comfortable with paid marketing tend to focus only on the channels that allow them to do this well. But what if you were to excel at using AdWords and community building? This again positions you uniquely to be knowledgeable about how to leverage an unusual combination of channels towards specific growth goals.

Seeing What Makes Growth Hackers Tick

Almost everything that gets written about a growth hacker's characteristics tends to focus on the skills they need to have in order to do their job. Skills can be learned by anyone with time and dedication. The more critical aspect, in my view, has to do with the behavioral characteristics and work styles of growth professionals. Again, in my view, that gets extremely short shrift, perhaps because it's anecdotal. This is unfortunate.

Just as having the wrong CEO can impact a company's ability to hit its business goals, someone who lacks the proper characteristics to lead growth similarly will not be able to execute a growth process effectively. This is important because when it comes to how we act at work, we all have *traits* — our habits, the way we think, and the way we react to situations. And every trait produces a drive to have certain things. These drives create needs, which in turn motivate us to behave in a way that satisfies those needs.

Measuring the impact of behavioral characteristics can be tricky. In my attempt to go beyond the anecdotal, I collected data from more than 30 growth leads. I used a workstyle behavioral assessment tool that's been in use for over 60 years as of this writing, created by the Predictive Index (PI). This tool has been used to quantify people's behavioral drives in the workplace in four areas (called *factors*) that provide an enormous amount of insight about how someone will behave at work.

These four factors are defined this way:

>> **Dominance:** The drive to exert one's influence on people or events

>> **Extraversion:** The drive for social interaction with other people

>> **Patience:** The drive for consistency and stability

>> **Formality:** The drive to conform to rules and structure

The results of the PI Behavioral Assessment, which are based on these four factors, can generate 17 different patterns (or *reference profiles*) that create a behavioral map for different types of people. You can think of these as easy-to-reference groupings of the characteristics of people who have similar drives. These patterns reveal which of the four factors is strongest, which tells you a lot about what it's like to work with that person. Figure 2-2 is an example of what one of these 17 reference profiles looks like.

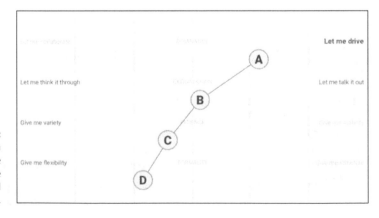

FIGURE 2-2: An example of a reference profile generated by the PI Behavioral Assessment.

Don't take reference profiles as gospel — people are complex, and everyone is unique. These specific profiles are not personality tests, either. They're merely one more way for you to get a deeper insight into preferred work styles. No profile is better than the other. However, certain profiles are better suited for certain kinds of roles based on the needs of that job.

I asked more than 30 former and current growth leads in my network from around the world (irrespective of their actual titles) to take this assessment. These are people who have led growth at a broad range of companies — from start-ups you may not have heard of yet but are scaling up fast to more well-known companies all the way up to a conglomerate with hundreds of thousands of employees. (Yes, they have growth teams, too!) I was also curious about Sean Ellis's pattern, so I asked him to take this assessment as well.

Though 30-plus growth leads is a relatively small sample, some commonalities emerged. Three reference profiles were the most common among this group — Maverick, Individualist, and Persuader, in the PI parlance.

Just because I'm focusing on the most common patterns that emerged from my survey doesn't mean that individuals who had other patterns don't make for effective growth leads. In some aspects, they share similar characteristics with the ones I talk about in the list below. Where larger differences emerge, those are more a reflection of different needs, behaviors, signature work styles, and strengths.

Looking at these three workstyles, the most common patterns that emerge (including the specific needs, behaviors, signature work styles, and strengths of each profile) are as described in this list:

>> **Maverick:** An innovative person who thinks outside the box and is undaunted by failure

- *Needs*

  Challenges

  Opportunities to influence

  Variety

  Freedom from rules and controls

- *Behaviors*

  Venturesome

  Enthusiastic

Driving

Tolerant of uncertainty

- *Signature work styles*

Communication: Forceful, direct, animated, telling

Delegation: Freely delegates with loose follow-up

Decision-making: Innovator, confident decision-maker

Action and risk: Quick to act and believes that risk is necessary and that "the ends justify the means"

- *Strengths*

Responds positively to challenges and pressure

A visionary who includes people in the planning

Goal-oriented

>> **Individualist:** A highly independent and persistent thinker who nevertheless remains results-oriented

- *Needs*

Independence

Opportunities to work with facts

Flexibility

Freedom from changing priorities

- *Behaviors*

Self-confident

Analytical

Methodical

Nonconforming

- *Signature work styles*

Communication: Directive, telling, factual, with strong conviction

Delegation: Delegates details

Decision-making: Creative problem-solver, decisive

Action and risk: Able to take risk, acts on new or unconventional ideas

- *Strengths*

  Drives change and challenges the status quo

  Creative problem-solver, goal-oriented

  Adept at handling changing organizational needs

» **Persuader:** A risk-taking, socially poised and motivating team builder

- *Needs*

  Independence

  Opportunities to interact with others

  Variety and change

  Freedom from rigid structure

- *Behaviors*

  Self-confident

  Persuasive, stimulating

  Fast-paced

  Informal

- *Signature work styles*

  Communication: Empathetic, persuasive selling style, gregarious, extraverted

  Delegation: Delegates authority and details

  Decision Making: Confident decision-maker, works through people to solve problems

  Action and risk: Venturesome risk-taker, strong initiative

- *Strengths*

  Drives change and challenges status quo

  Motivating, stimulating communicator

  Proactive and results-oriented

Simply reading these three profile summaries should indicate some commonalities between these profiles, and a few differences too.

If you visualize the key words in the summaries as a word cloud, you see the result shown in Figure 2-3.

FIGURE 2-3:
Key traits and
strengths of
growth leads.

The words that immediately pop out are ones like opportunities, change, challenges, and delegates, but also results-oriented, freedom, decision-maker, and problem-solver. All this makes sense, but instead of it being anecdotal, for the first time you have a data-informed set of traits to look for, along with the right skill set to look for if you plan to hire a growth lead.

IN THIS CHAPTER

» Seeing why you need a growth team

» Determining the team roles you need to fill

» Starting a growth team

» Finding a place for your growth team in your organizational structure

» Looking at how growth leads impact team dynamics

Chapter **3**

Building Growth Teams

So you've decided that you need growth hackers as part of your organization. After making that decision, the next thing you have to figure out is how to get those growth hackers to work effectively together. This task tends to take the form of a growth team, perhaps loosely defined at first and then with more formal roles as the organization matures. Whatever the state of the growth team, its purpose remains the same: to grow usage of your product as a function of growing the value you deliver. You do this by finding repeatable and sustainable levers of growth by continually examining your growth model for opportunities or problems.

Folks often say to me, "Hey, I already have a growth hacker working for me. Why do I need a team?" The answer, quite simply, is math. No single person has all the answers. Even when it comes to brainstorming ideas to test, a team will naturally have more than one person. And, especially when you want a culture of growth to permeate the entire company, you cannot have a situation where you have one person sitting in the corner doing "that growth hacking stuff" while everybody else continues doing what they do. A cross-functional team helps spread the message to all corners of the organization to get everyone else excited about participating in the growth process.

Growth hacking is all about focusing on the entire customer journey, whereas traditional marketing is about getting people to the product, and product development concentrates on making a product that people want to use. Those distinctions show that product and marketing teams as defined lack the ability to help scale your product. You need something else to bridge the divide, and a growth team is the answer.

A *growth team* uses quantitative and qualitative data to understand what stands in the way when it comes to customers experiencing the value of your product, whether that roadblock occurs in an acquisition channel or within the first product experience. So, for most of what the growth team will do, you need people from different roles — product, marketing, sales, engineering, data, operations, and so on — as part of your growth team.

REMEMBER

A growth team can't create value where there is none. The focus is to grow the value of, and find more customers for, a product that has already found product-market fit through a process of data-informed, high-tempo testing.

Investigating Growth Team Structure

When I was at GrowthHackers, we functionally mirrored a core team structure that Sean Ellis had seen at many other organizations, including these roles:

>> **Growth lead:** Known by a variety of other titles such as growth PM, head of growth, and variations thereof, the growth lead is responsible for driving growth for the product and spreading the growth culture throughout the organization. This person investigates growth models, sets objectives, runs the weekly growth meeting, and generally keeps tabs on ongoing progress. Other than having mastered the skill set needed for a successful growth hacker — see Chapter 2 for more on that topic — this person is also a strong leader and manager.

>> **Growth engineer:** If there's one person you will likely need before any other in order to actually launch tests, it's this one. They will do everything from coding features to creating analytics events for measuring the impact of tests for your team. (Analytics events are user interactions that can be measured from a web page or a screen load.) Ideally, this is a full-stack engineer who is able to deal with front-end and back-end technicalities. The most non-obvious characteristic of an engineer is that, because the person has technical knowledge, when they understand the setup needs for a test, often they can come up with more elegant ways to construct and/or launch a test than someone (like me) who has minimal technical skills.

REMEMBER

The best growth engineer is someone who is quite comfortable with having their work "thrown away." This is important, given that most tests end up failing. So, having someone who isn't as wedded to their work as much as they are wedded to the insights gained from their work is essential.

>> **Growth designer:** Though the ethos of "getting it done is better than getting it perfect" is perfectly appropriate in many aspects of life, when it comes to launching tests, you don't want to launch ones that are not representative of the product or brand experience. Employing a growth designer is a necessary check to ensure that tests not only have an appropriate look and feel but also provide user insights. This ensures that the experience of the test is one that's aligned with the insights you're trying to extract from the test. And, of course, because they're on the growth team, growth designers need to move faster through the design-and-approval process, given that tests need to be launched on a weekly (or biweekly) schedule. So, other than the growth engineer, you'll find that this role, because of its specialized nature, will be one you'll find essential.

>> **Marketing specialist:** One primary job of a growth hacker (and, indeed, the growth team as a whole) is to continually test within channels in order to find ways to scale acquisition. The decision of who takes on this role is almost always driven by which channels are working. So, if Facebook Ads are working best right now, the person in this role should be a specialist who knows that platform inside and out so that you're able to squeeze the maximum amount of growth out of its potential.

You may also consider this role to be more "plug and play," where different individuals take on this role as circumstances change. Given that the efficiency of channels will continue evolving, growth teams will also be testing newer channels. If no expertise exists in-house to even test the potential of some new channels, you can supplement the in-house marketing person with specialists (individual freelancers or agencies) to focus on those channels to prove them out (or not). Alternately, if there is no marketer on the team yet, you can start by contracting such a specialist. It'll be quicker to get started with testing that way. If these channels do show potential, maybe that makes the case for hiring someone full-time to focus on that channel and/or also keep working with the external specialist for the long term.

>> **Data analyst:** You may not have a dedicated person for this role when you start, but you do need someone who is responsible for analyzing tests and extracting insights to inform future actions. This person needs to understand analytics systems, connect disparate data sources, be able to ask good questions, and generate reports that can answer those questions.

You want answers to questions based on the hypotheses your tests set out to prove, but you also want answers to questions that impact the larger business.

Having a data analyst onboard doesn't mean that the rest of the growth team is absolved of the responsibility of understanding data. In fact, it's useful to have others on the team ask whether the analyst has considered specific aspects of the data when coming to their conclusions.

TIP

Growth teams are all about breaking silos and aligning the entire company around the NSM, so though the core team will resemble the one I just summarized, you need representation from other groups to help the mission. Key stakeholders from product, sales, and any other key departments of the company should be in the loop and represented at growth meetings to ensure that everyone is on board with — or has flagged potential concerns in a timely fashion with — whatever the growth team prioritizes on an ongoing basis.

It's also important to realize that growth teams, with the core team roles I just summarized, aren't how most teams start out. In many cases, growth teams start out organically as just one person informally leading a bunch of people who report to their respective line managers but are brought together to understand and solve growth problems. Over time, they evolve into growth teams with more formal roles. If you're reading this book, your experience with growth teams is likely one where you're getting one off the ground or are formalizing one. It's the rarer situation that a company has a large growth team that is broken into subgroups, with some focusing on making large bets and others focusing on optimizing different parts of the customer lifecycle.

Getting a growth team off the ground

You can't just decide one day, "Hey, today is the day I start my growth team." The impact of this team is sure to cut across multiple departments, so before you get going, you need to have their buy-in. The ideal way to do that is to convince someone from the executive team of the merits and need for this team. Ideally, it's the CEO or a founder, but the person in senior management who leads a product or marketing team would work as well. This is the person who will champion the team and evangelize your wins.

The biggest reason for getting buy-in is that the growth team will carry out tasks that impact the product, which is someone else's ultimate responsibility. The product team will already have in place a development process and priorities that have likely been planned out for weeks and months in advance. What you're proposing is having your growth team come in and "try things" on a rapid schedule and advocate for making product changes that have not been on the roadmap previously. You can imagine that the product team wouldn't be overly happy about this. And even if you have strong support from the senior management team, that doesn't absolve the growth team of the responsibility of building individual support on other teams in order to show the true value of what the growth team will do and find ways to mitigate tensions when it comes to making changes in the product as a result of new findings.

Similarly, the growth team may be trying things within acquisition channels or in terms of the product itself that test the boundaries of what is considered to be "on brand." This, too, will cause understandable nervousness among those responsible for maintaining the brand experience. Having them onboard is critical to having them be open to tests that deviate from the established brand voice and style.

When you're first getting a growth team off the ground — especially when you're doing that at a start-up in its very early stage — the "head of growth" is likely to be the CEO or a founder. At other times, it's a product leader or even the first marketer, as was the case with Sean Ellis at Dropbox. In either case, the growth team is in actuality just the one person using some marketing technology to run tests and also convincing other people in the organization to help. These individuals will likely come from the product marketing, user experience design, brand, and engineering teams. You'll need to flex some of your influencing skills here to generate excitement about what you're trying to do so that you can get these people to spare an hour or two (or three) of their time to help launch the test. If that doesn't work, you can always persuade your executive team champion to get some time from these people. But this situation generally doesn't last long.

WARNING

Be picky about whom you ask for help. A person who may be enthusiastic but have no time or someone who may not be able to work as fast as you need to can stall your efforts prematurely. If you have to (and have the ability to), use freelancers to achieve what you otherwise couldn't with in-house assistance.

Early teams like these often find that continually having to beg for resources hinders the ability to act on growth challenges. To allow such a team to function relatively independently, this team needs two other people: a growth engineer and a growth designer. Such a team can tackle a variety of problems across the customer journey without much difficulty because analytics can now be put in place to measure the impact of tests, snippets of code needed for tests can be implemented, and tests that represent the product/brand experience can be launched at a fast pace.

After this team hits its stride and starts to show wins, you're in a position to interrogate your growth model and start building a testing culture, which, if you recall, are integral parts of the job for whoever you have leading growth. If that person isn't a marketer, a majority of these tests are likely being done within the product experience as opposed to acquisition channels, which means that the next person you'll probably want to add to the team is a marketer so that you can start to scale acquisition (the third big part of the job for your growth lead).

If the marketer is the person leading growth, perhaps they've already begun testing channels that can scale. If you're lucky, one channel that shows promise is the one in which the marketer has expertise. If not, it's time to bring onboard the person with the right skills so that future tests can start to have broad-based impact throughout the customer journey.

As you start to get more robust with your testing, your need for better experimentation infrastructure and analytics will increase proportionately. This is when you should start looking for a data analyst to add to the team. You may also find that you need more than one growth engineer to tackle whatever problem or opportunity your testing uncovers. (It's a fact of life that different technologies — web versus Android versus iOS, for example — require different skills.) As long as you let the data and the follow-up resources needed to launch tests determine who should be brought on next to the growth team, you'll find that you'll have little problem in justifying their being hired.

Seeing who answers to whom

In 2015, Andrew McInnes (entrepreneur-in-residence at Bionic) and Daisuke Miyoshi (growth marketer at Tradecraft) interviewed 20 growth leads and unearthed two methods for structuring a growth team:

>> Independent-led model (Facebook, Uber)

>> Functional model (LinkedIn, Dropbox)

In the independent-led model, the growth team is its own department and reports to a senior executive, who reports directly to the CEO. Obviously, this structure is more autonomous but is difficult to implement if not done early. This structure does lend itself to speed and being able to iterate constantly, which can be assets if that's what the company culture values as well.

Two variations of the independent-led model emerged from McInnes and Miyoshi's research — one organized by flows and features (shown in Figure 3-1) and another by metrics that mapped to the user lifecycle (shown in Figure 3-2).

The obvious trap with the independent-led model is that, if it proves unable to establish trust and a working relationship with the heads of the other key groups, the growth team may find itself struggling for acceptance and support. So, the head of growth has to work doubly hard here in order to ensure strong alignment with growth activities and other key initiatives throughout the organization.

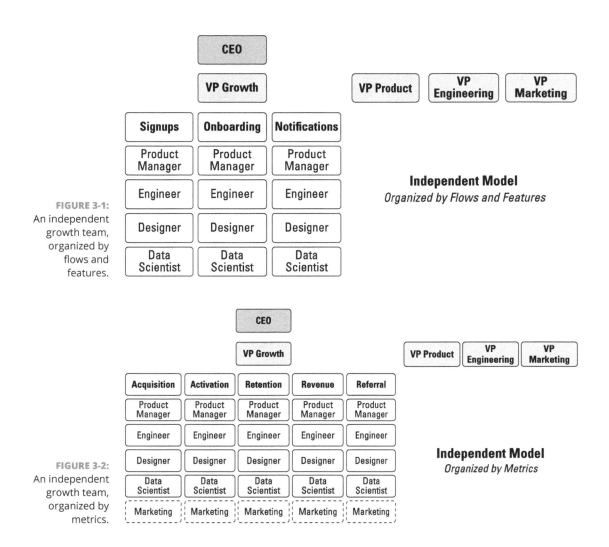

FIGURE 3-1:
An independent growth team, organized by flows and features.

Independent Model
Organized by Flows and Features

FIGURE 3-2:
An independent growth team, organized by metrics.

Independent Model
Organized by Metrics

In a functional model, the growth team reports to the senior executive in charge, more often than not, of product management. (See Figure 3-3.) Based on direction and agreement with this executive, the growth lead targets specific initiatives on an ongoing basis.

This reporting structure may make it seem as though growth initiatives are being balanced with nongrowth initiatives, resulting in a slowing down of what the growth team can try. But in reality, the person in charge of product development is accounting for key performance indicators (KPIs) for growth in their plan and ensuring appropriate prioritizations and resources as part of their planning. This means that other department heads are brought on board to agree on these initiatives early as part of some type of matrixed reporting structure, leading to less conflict than what you might potentially see with the independent model.

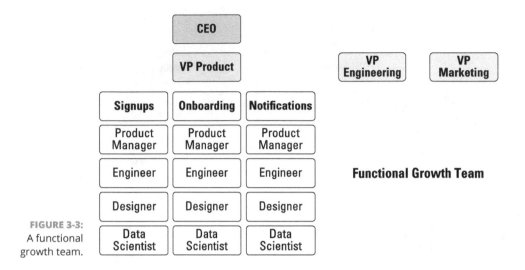

FIGURE 3-3:
A functional
growth team.

When a growth team hasn't been formed early in a company's life, the functional model is the more common scenario because company culture has had more time to set, and organizational processes have already been established.

A critical finding of the research that unearthed these models also showed that there is no significant difference when it comes to the impact of picking between the two models. This, again, goes back to the point that the model you pick is more a function of your company culture than anything else. You may find that neither of these works for you and some hybrid of the two fits best.

TIP

A good way to think about which model might work best may be to investigate the growth model for where the biggest opportunities (or problems) may lie and let that guide discussions and decisions on what organizational structure may be best suited to tackle those particular opportunities (or problems).

REMEMBER

Whatever the structure, unless the executive team has bought into the need for a growth team, it's doomed to fail, no matter which model you pick.

Gauging the Impact of Growth Leads

Almost everything that gets written about the characteristics of growth leads tends to be from the perspective of the individual. However, given the outsized impact of this individual on how the growth team operates (and their impact back on company culture), it seems odd that almost nothing of consequence is written about how growth leads impact how growth teams work together, how they communicate, how they take action, and how they make decisions. This is a glaring omission, given that so much is said about the culture of the company impacting the growth team. The culture of the growth team itself is just as important because no growth process can be executed effectively without this team operating efficiently.

If growth is about being data-informed, you should be as data-informed about growth team dynamics as you are about your growth metrics. So, I set out to do some research for this chapter to visualize how growth leads impact teamwork styles and behaviors.

For this, I used the Team Work Styles tool provided by the Predictive Index, which is built for exactly this purpose. The reports from this tool can help you understand the impact of the growth lead on the team's behavioral dynamics. Before I show you what I came up with, however, it's a good idea to look at organizational cultures in a broader context. If that sounds useful, read the next section.

Looking at the Four Types of Organizational Cultures

The Competing Values framework, developed in the early 1980s by Robert E. Quinn and John Rohrbaugh, has been used quite extensively as a model of organizational culture. This model tries to describe how opposing drives (also known as competing values) show up in organizations.

The findings of Quinn and Rohrbaugh indicate two major types of competing values:

>> **Stability versus flexibility:** When the organization prioritizes stability, order, and control as opposed to flexibility, innovation, and change

>> **Internally focused versus externally focused:** When the organization prioritizes employee needs and company processes as opposed to prioritizing being more competitive and focusing on client needs

Quinn and Rohrbaugh used a 4-quadrant design to show where organizations fall on these sets of values. The Predictive Index uses this same framework to identify four common organizational cultures, as shown in Figure 3-4:

>> **Cultivating:** Rewards cooperation, collaboration, and patience. The teams in a cultivating organization focus on teamwork and relationship-building.

>> **Exploring:** Rewards challenging the status quo and executing in the face of uncertainty. Teams in an exploring organization focus on innovation and agility.

>> **Producing:** Rewards a bias toward action and driving forward, no matter what. Teams in a producing organization focus on results and discipline.

>> **Stabilizing:** Rewards a conservative approach, reliability, diligence, and consistency with the output. Teams in a stabilizing organization focus on process and precision.

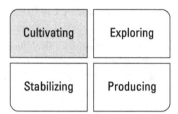

FIGURE 3-4:
The four major organizational cultures.

If you revisualize these four organizational cultures from the perspective of their foci, it looks like Figure 3-5.

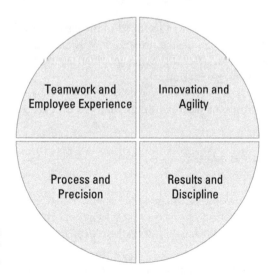

FIGURE 3-5:
The four major foci of teams.

REMEMBER

Though organizations commonly promote more than one type of culture, one culture may be more important than others, either companywide or within a team at a particular point in time as a way to ensure that the team can execute on its strategic priorities.

From the perspective of growth teams, the team leader is ultimately responsible for unlocking avenues of sustainable growth. This means that this person is the one who has to promote a culture that continually and rapidly tests across the customer journey to learn about activities that can be systemized as processes to grow the value that a business provides its customers.

Determining the overall impact of specific organizational cultures

If you had to come up with an initial hypothesis of what kind of culture a growth lead might want to promote these days, you'd likely say that the person would be pushing for innovation and agility. That's the culture that rewards moving fast and finding new ways to drive sustainable growth via constant testing.

When I mapped the behavioral work styles of 31 growth leads onto this construct, I indeed saw that most of them fall into, or straddle, this Innovation and Agility quadrant, as shown in Figure 3-6.

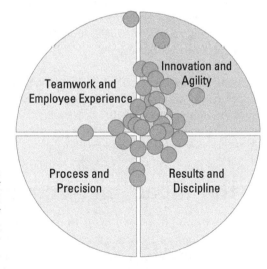

FIGURE 3-6: Distribution of behavioral profiles of 31 current and former growth leads.

REMEMBER

I am not implying in any way that people who fall outside the Innovation and Agility quadrant don't make good growth leads. This reflects only the kind of culture they tend to gravitate toward, not that they can't or don't operate in other ways.

Seeing that a majority of growth leads fall into the Innovation and Agility quadrant, however, is to be expected because their behavioral work styles indicate that they are Mavericks, Individualists, and Persuaders. (For more on these characterizations. see Chapter 2.)

From an overall perspective, based on the quadrant that most growth leads fall into, you can tell that they're risk-takers who are out to make an impact by being extremely creative and entrepreneurial. Their strengths are being ambitious and goal-oriented, being able to adapt to changing circumstances quickly, and thriving under pressure.

On the flip side, this drive makes growth leads extremely impatient and pushes them to continually seek action. They're generally not as detail oriented, choosing to focus more on progress than anything else. So, though growth leads may provide ample opportunities to tackle big problems, if they treat every team member as a version of themselves, they may start to micromanage the team versus giving them the space they need to execute and see results.

TIP

Here's one way to avoid the micromanaging trap: Whenever your growth leads find themselves growing impatient, they should ask specific questions about plans and details that are being considered — even plans and details that they may not care about but others on the team might. This allows them a better understanding of the time and amount of work needed for tasks, lets them perhaps gain agreement on things that need to take more time (or that could be sped up), and allows them to calibrate their expectations accordingly.

REMEMBER

The culture that the growth lead promotes has a major impact on how team members work together, specifically when it comes to how the team communicates, takes action, and makes decisions. These aptitudes are generally taken for granted or are not optimized for, leading to situations where growth teams are not being able to execute on their strategic priorities effectively.

Recognizing the impact on communication

My research for this chapter on how growth leads impact team work styles and behaviors also took a closer look at how work styles specifically impact team communication. Here, the distribution on my Organizational Cultures quadrant wasn't as clear-cut. I found that a majority of my growth leads straddled two different communication styles — the Telling and Persuading styles — with about an equal number falling within the boundaries of these two styles. (See Figure 3-7.)

The Telling style is all about having your opinions coming out loud and fast. Such growth leads are assertive, get to the point, and move on quickly and efficiently. Being authoritative and factual are hallmarks of their communication styles.

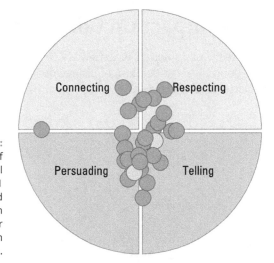

REMEMBER

FIGURE 3-7:
Distribution of
behavioral
profiles of 31
current and
former growth
leads and their
impact on
communication.

To some team members, this can come across as quite rough. Such growth leads are so confident in their own judgment that they may find it difficult to even consider listening to what other team members have to say — without even realizing it.

The way successful growth leads with such a communication style have managed to find their way around such traps is to be more conscious of their tone but also coaching the rest of the team to provide more facts or information that help them understand what the team is doing. Structured communications with team members, like weekly emails with key bullet points and/or weekly one-on-ones, ensure that everyone is on track and on the same page.

The Persuading style, though also about talking fast and energetically, is more about influencing the team and building support. Growth leads who are persuaders are articulate and excel at building rapport and motivating team members to action.

Something to watch out for with this communication style is that it may still come across as rushed and haphazard. But despite their need to move fast, such growth leads may waste time listening to arguments that are clearly wrong-headed, if they come up just to preserve team harmony. And even after spending that time, they may still not take no for an answer and work hard to impress their views on the team.

Because such leads are (fast) talkers and all about influencing their team, they do have to be actively reminded to listen to other opinions. Constraining communication to key headlines and bullet points to show how tasks connect to goals is helpful to them as well.

Evaluating the impact on taking action

Clearly, how a growth team takes action is extremely important to its success. Here, the distribution along the Organizational Cultures quadrant was clearer and mirrored the overall pattern. (See Figure 3-8.)

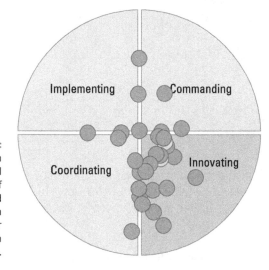

FIGURE 3-8:
Distribution
of behavioral
profiles of
31 current and
former growth
leads and their
impact on
taking action.

The Innovating style is all about challenging the status quo, doing things quickly, and driving forward in new and creative ways. Just as you saw with the overall impact on dynamics, such growth leads are highly adaptable, love taking charge, and thrive on the pressure of the job.

They put a lot of stock in their own judgment and are more concerned with action and progress over execution details or being completely in line with rules or processes.

The way such growth leads have been able to succeed is by being good about delegating the tasks they may not care about to other team members wherever possible. And, though growth teams generally need a lack of constraints in order to execute effectively, such teams are even more explicit about when rules have to be followed and have made it a part of their operating procedure to ensure compliance when deciding on what to do — and what not to do.

Seeing the impact on decision-making

The growth team is nothing if not about moving fast. After all, they're prepping, launching, and learning from tests all the time. When I looked at the impact of growth leads on how teams make decisions, again, a majority pattern emerged — the Justifying style, shown in Figure 3-9.

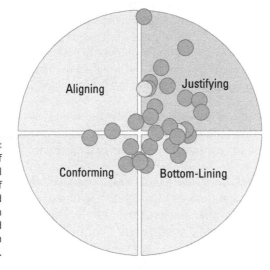

With the Justifying style, growth leads encourage everyone to have an opinion and to express it, especially when it comes to being vocal about challenging the status quo so that the team can arrive at the best decision. Such growth leads are tolerant of risk and conflict. They're good about recognizing how decisions impact others.

Despite this, they may still need additional help understanding how actions they approve may impact the bigger picture. Because of the predisposition to action, the run the risk of misalignment with other teams, and they may not like their decisions being questioned in such cases.

Such growth leads improve the presentation of opinions and ideas by introducing mechanisms to vote on them before acting on anything. They also build in processes to ensure that the risks they may take are evaluated appropriately before they're acted on and to also course-correct if issues are perceived later.

Strategic Priorities of Growth Teams

Earlier in the chapter I show you the distribution of growth leads and how a majority fell into the Innovation and Agility quadrant of the Team Work Styles report from The Predictive Index. Now, I know from my own experience that if all growth teams focused only on this quadrant, they would not be very successful.

As an example, consider what you read in the first paragraph about growth hacking being a process. This process is necessary to provide focus to the speed that the team wants to move at. But as you see from the Team Work Styles report quadrants (refer to Figure 3-5), the Process and Precision quadrant is diametrically opposite to the Innovation and Agility quadrant. Then remember what you've already read about growth being a cross-functional process that breaks down silos. This speaks to the Teamwork and Employee Experience quadrant. And lastly, growth teams are very results-oriented and use data to inform where they should focus. So here we find representation from the "Results and Discipline" quadrant.

Intuitively and from personal experience this makes sense, but I surveyed the very same growth leads that took the PI Behavioral assessments so I could also show what they considered to be strategic priorities of their teams.

Again, I used the Team Work Styles tool, which has a strategic priorities overlay with 5 priorities per quadrants (see Figure 3-10), to find out where the overlap (or lack thereof) was between the inherent work style strengths of growth leads and what they indicated as strategic priorities for their teams

From the 20 priorities available, I asked them to choose the 5 to 8 activities that were most critical to the success of their growth team. They did not have to pick priorities from quadrants that did not apply if that were the case. I did not give them any more description of the priorities other than the titles you see in Figure 3-10 as they're simple and self-explanatory.

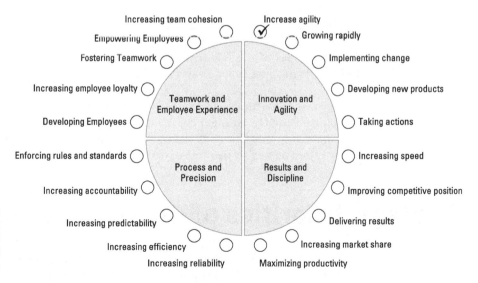

FIGURE 3-10: Strategic priorities overlaid on Team Work Style quadrants.

At first glance, what was interesting to see is that, on an aggregate basis, every option had at least one person selecting it. This could be a function of company stage and/or vertical. Also, no one picked less than 5 priorities as per the instructions. As expected, though, some priorities were clearly more important than others when tallying the totals. Figure 3-11 shows the top 8 priorities across the board, which (as I expected) are evenly scattered across all quadrants:

>> **Innovation & Agility quadrant:** Increasing agility and growing rapidly

>> **Teamwork & Employee Experience quadrant:** Empowering employees and developing employees ("employees" is a stand-in for team members in the case of the growth team)

>> **Process & Precision quadrant:** Increasing accountability and increasing efficiency

>> **Results & Discipline quadrant:** Delivering results and increasing speed

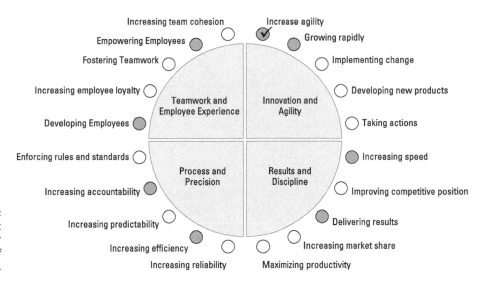

FIGURE 3-11: Top strategic priorities for growth teams of 31 growth leads.

This leads us to some interesting conclusions. On the one hand, we have growth leads that for the most part fall into the Innovation and Agility quadrant because of the behavioral work styles they tend to display. But at the same time, as leaders, they can't simply work the way they are naturally inclined to. The strategic priorities of the team go beyond what they are naturally best suited for. This means that if the team is going to achieve its strategic priorities, growth leads cannot have everyone on the team be just like them. That is a recipe for failure. They also clearly need to be working to develop themselves as leaders to ensure that their team is always functioning at a high level.

They need to be mindful that, because they may have priorities that don't align with their natural work style strengths, they need to have people on the team with complementary work styles if you want the team to achieve those goals. As an example, when hiring a data analyst, they might want to consider someone whose strengths fall within the Results and Discipline quadrant to ensure that the team is making the best decisions based on accurate data analysis. You also read earlier in the chapter about engineers being comfortable with moving fast and constantly changing direction. In this case, engineers who are more like growth leads in their work style could be very beneficial.

You take this approach of evaluating every team member's work style and its impact on the team and ability to execute on strategic priorities until you end up with a team that is optimized to work on growth initiatives.

2

Seeing Where Growth Opportunities Come From

Chapter **4**

Applying Customer Journey Frameworks

The customer journey is the path that someone who knows nothing about your product takes in order to find — and then use — your product. In this chapter, I lay out the importance of visualizing this concept so that you can grow your product. I also introduce the frameworks, tools, and methods that will help you understand the customer journey of your own product.

Visualizing the customer for your product lays the foundation for you to collect data and audit the current state of your product's growth. This is ammunition you can use to go back to key stakeholders and have a data-informed discussion about what it would take to grow your product. It also allows executives to understand gaps that could impact their plans for growth and help build the case to allocate resources to cover for those deficiencies. Lastly, knowing more about your customers means that you'll be not only better informed about what it will take to meet your current business goals but also better able to come away with recommendations on potential opportunities or problem areas that the team absolutely must pay attention to, to be able to achieve those goals. This in turn allows everyone to have a better discussion about the business's growth strategy as well as the associated challenges moving forward.

Understanding Customer Journey Frameworks

A *customer journey* is the collection of experiences a customer has when interacting with your product or brand. It takes into account every step from when a customer first hears about your product to realizing the value of your product and, ideally, becoming an advocate of your product.

Growth hacking is all about understanding where the biggest opportunities lie within that journey to grow the value you provide to your customers. To understand where such opportunities lie, you need to visualize how customers get to that value. A *customer journey framework* is a system to help you visualize customers' experiences with your product or brand. Once you've visualized their journey, you can analyze how they complete each step of that journey. This analysis in turn helps you understand more about how you can better help them through each step of that journey. This (repeatable) process allows you to improve at growing the value you provide as they take more turns experiencing the value your product provides.

WARNING

If you Google the term *customer journey framework,* you'll see that people have come up with multiple ways to visualize this concept. My problem with most of them is that they can be too detailed or complicated for people with zero experience with growth or marketing. The frameworks I kept coming back to are ones that allowed me to focus on just a few important concepts and keep moving forward. As in all areas of growth hacking, you have to find a balance between getting things done and gaining an in-depth understanding of a topic.

The two frameworks I've found to be most useful when getting started are the Pirate Metrics and Marketing Hourglass frameworks. As you'll soon see, both of them do an excellent job of providing you with the big picture of the customer journey. This is important when starting out, because drilling down into detail without this macro view may cause you to miss, or misidentify, where your biggest growth opportunities may lie.

Applying Pirate Metrics (also known as AARRR)

In 2007, Dave McClure, a co-founder of the start-up accelerator known as 500 Start-ups, changed how start-ups thought about the customer journey. He presented a simple framework he called Pirate Metrics (you'll see in a moment why he came up with that name). The framework had five steps, called Acquisition,

Activation, Retention, Referral, and Revenue. Because the mnemonic (or memory aid) for it literally was "AARRR"— the clichéd pirate expression from numerous books and movies — McClure felt that the term "Pirate Metrics" was a fitting one. It still is one of the most commonly referred-to frameworks for how start-ups think about key steps in the customer journey and how to optimize for them.

Acquisition, Activation, Retention, Referral, and Revenue are, as described by the questions in this list:

>> **Acquisition:** How are your prospective customers finding out about your product?

>> **Activation:** What convinces your prospective customer of the value of your product?

>> **Retention:** How do your customers continue experiencing the value of your product?

>> **Referral:** What gets your customers to talk about your product with others?

>> **Revenue:** What gets your customers to pay for your product?

McClure visualized these steps as a funnel to communicate the idea that as people work their way through each stage, fewer and fewer people make their way to the end of that journey. (See Figure 4-1.)

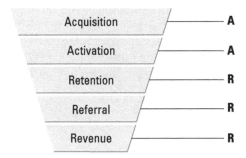

FIGURE 4-1:
Dave McClure's
Pirate Metrics.

TIP

Depending on the kind of product you sell, the position of Referral and Revenue in your funnel can be different. For example, a food delivery app may provide a referral code only after you've had a great experience that you've paid for.

Knowing how many people completed each stage gives you a macro picture of conversion rates and points to the part(s) of the journey where people are having difficulty realizing their true potential as customers. The advantage of this approach is that it focuses you on a subset of numbers that you absolutely must track and influence if your product is to deliver on its promised value.

You learn more in Chapter 6 about the process of understanding how your business grows and finding areas of your biggest growth opportunities.

WARNING

A downside of McClure's approach was that it lacked nuance — perhaps intentionally — for the sake of understanding his central point. It didn't take into account that the relative difficulty of making it from one step of the journey to the next may be different based on which steps you're talking about. Fortunately, another framework can help you understand this better.

Applying the Marketing Hourglass

John Jantsch, the creator of the Duct Tape Marketing System, came up with the concept of the Marketing Hourglass to address the fact that convincing people that your solution is the one they need is the toughest part of the journey. If you can do that, everything becomes easier from there on out. He envisioned this as an hourglass where, just like a funnel, you could have a lot of people showing up and checking out your product, but fewer people would end up trying it. This represented the small neck of the hourglass. If people tried it and it was the right solution for them, you would have no problem persuading them to pay for and talk about your product.

Jantsch, helpfully, labeled each step of his process with easy-to-understand words, such as *know, like, trust, try, buy, repeat,* and *refer.*

The key difference between McClure's approach and Jantsch's approach is that the former is envisioned as a series of sequentially decreasing conversion rates that you can optimize, whereas the latter is meant to depict the increasing opportunity to create an advocate once they've decided to give your product a shot. He used an image similar to the one shown in Figure 4-2 to represent the Marketing Hourglass.

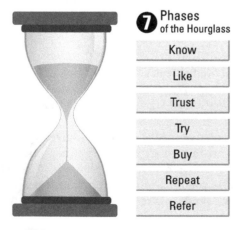

FIGURE 4-2: John Jantsch's Marketing Hourglass.

It's fairly easy to tell that there are similarities in the words used to describe McClure's Pirate Metrics and the stages of Jantsch's Marketing Hourglass. You can see the two frameworks superimposed in Table 4-1.

TABLE 4-1

Pirate Metrics and Marketing Hourglass, Superimposed

AARRR Start-up Metrics	Marketing Hourglass
Acquisition	Know
Activation	Like, trust, try
Revenue*	Buy
Retention	Repeat
Referral	Refer*

*The position of Revenue is interchangeable based on the business.

The reality, however, is that neither of these frameworks gives you the complete picture of the customer journey.

Both frameworks — among other, similar ones — make it easy to understand key points in the customer journey. Their effectiveness in doing so is beyond question, given how often they're quoted and used years after their introduction.

The problem with these oversimplified views is twofold:

>> **Unidirectional:** Despite the last steps of these frameworks being the act of referring your product to others, they're visually depicted as unidirectional. If customers are going to refer someone, then referrals become, by definition, another way that people find out about your product. This suggests that the visual representation should be more like a loop than a funnel.

This absence of visual element connecting the referral step to the acquisition step strengthens the implication of this 1-way traffic nature of the frameworks. If you connect the loop, it provides a better understanding of how the end of one journey enables the start of another and what you need to do to enable it. (See Figure 4-3.)

>> **Blind to nonlinearity:** Think about the last time you bought something online. How much research did you do? How many tabs did you have to open during that research? How many review sites did you visit? Did you also ask any friends what they thought? And then did you make your purchase during the first visit to the product site? The reality is that, more often than not, your customer journey is more of a zigzag than a straight line. (See Figure 4-4.)

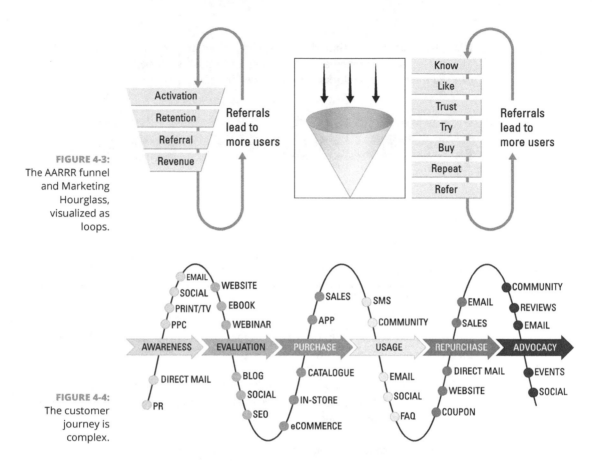

FIGURE 4-3: The AARRR funnel and Marketing Hourglass, visualized as loops.

FIGURE 4-4: The customer journey is complex.

These frameworks help with understanding the key points of a customer journey, but fall short of communicating the actual reality of that journey.

REMEMBER

Using Tools to Visualize Customer Journeys

The axiom "What gets measured gets managed" has never been truer. If anything, you could now say, "What gets measured gets grown." Marketing technology companies have taken this to heart. As of this writing, according to the latest Marketing Technology Landscape visualized by Scott Brinker, you can pick from hundreds of analytics and data visualization tools. For our purposes, however, there are just two types of tools to pay attention to first — aggregate user analytics and behavioral analytics.

Understanding aggregate user analytics

Aggregate data is, as the name suggests, data available as a collection. You've encountered this in real-life in the form of vote counts for elections or unemployment rates, for example. In both cases, individual data points (data about individual people, in other words) are collated and reported. The important thing is that the individual people themselves are never personally identified in these reports. Individual data points can also be combined in different ways to present new insights. For example, election counts could be in the form of city-wide, district-wide or state-wide results, which can then be further sliced by demographic characteristics to show more granular regions of support for a candidate.

This is exactly how aggregate user analytics works. Individual data points representing people's activities on your site are combined to present a picture of how people as a whole behave on your site. Users are not identified personally but other characteristics can be combined to give you an idea of the kinds of people you are attracting to your product and how they behave.

Google Analytics, a free tool provided by Google, is the most popular analytics tool used for this purpose. It gives you insight into how people find and use your website. Like almost every analytics tool now available, Google Analytics is easy to set up if you have the technical know-how.

Follow these basic steps for installation:

1. **Create an analytics account (or log into an existing one) at** https:// google.com/analytics.

2. **On the Admin tab of the page that appears, click the Tracking Info link to find the tracking code.**

3. **Copy and paste this code onto all pages of your website before the closing </head> tag. (See Figure 4-5.)**

TIP

If your organization is already using Google Tag Manager, you can install Google Analytics within Google Tag Manager.

After you've performed these actions, Google Analytics is ready to start recording what is happening on your site.

You're now ready to review the main aspects of Google Analytics and set up goals to track your site's successes. I discuss this topic more over the next few pages.

This is your tracking code. Copy and paste it into the code of every page you want to track.

```
<script>
(function(i,s,o,g,r,a,m){i['GoogleAnalyticsObject']=r;i[r]=i[r]||function(){
(i[r].q=i[r].q||[]).push(arguments)},i[r].l=1*new Date();a=s.createElement(o),
m=s.getElementsByTagName(o)[0];a.async=1;a.src=g;m.parentNode.insertBefore(a,m)
})(window,document,'script','//www.google-analytics.com/analytics.js','ga');

ga('create', 'UA-23929748-3', 'ianslofgren.com');
ga('send', 'pageview');

</script>
```

FIGURE 4-5:
A Google
Analytics
JavaScript
snippet.

In general, your website serves as one of the main hubs, if not *the* main hub, of information for your product. You will likely send people to various parts of your site by way of various campaigns to learn more about — and, hopefully, buy (or download or sign up for) — your product. Google Analytics helps you track and measure the effectiveness of your site.

REMEMBER

Google Analytics doesn't identify individuals, and so its utility lies in providing aggregate data. It does so by presenting information in three main buckets that also represent the customer journey, as described in this list:

>> **Acquisition:** This section provides information on how people find out about and come to your site — how you acquire traffic, in other words. The reports here help you identify all the sources of traffic and which ones contribute most to your business goals over time. (See Figure 4-6.)

>> **Behavior:** This section tells you what people do after they arrive at your website. You can then see whether they are doing the things you want them to do or are getting stuck somewhere. You can use this information to make changes to the flow of your site and make it easier for people to derive value from your product. One of my favorite parts of this section is Behavior Flow view, where, again, in aggregate you can see every step of the journey and how it branches through the site. This makes it easy to quickly identify areas of trouble or opportunity.

>> **Conversion:** This section tells you how you're doing with achieving business goals, which are typically converting visitors into customer. It provides more data that adds on to the Behavior data to draw a complete picture of what people had to experience in order to convert — whatever that means in your context.

FIGURE 4-6:
Google Analytics
Acquisition
overview.

WARNING

When you encounter Google Analytics for the first time, it's easy to be wowed by all the information it spits out by default and then to be satisfied with that. But it doesn't reveal its true power without some work on your part to analyze the data for insights. This work falls into two categories: goals and funnels.

Goals

Goals are a way of measuring how well your site or app fulfills your target objectives. A goal within the software measures whether a key activity in the growth of your product took place. The goal forms the foundation of what you measure and informs actions you might take in the future to grow key numbers that matter. It goes without saying, then, that you need to have at least a good hypothesis of which key actions you might want to measure — if you don't already know them.

In this context, a goal might be to have visitors sign up to try your product as a result of an advertising campaign or to have them click on an email link to return and engage again on your site or to have them buy a product from an ecommerce site. (See Figure 4-7.)

Goals let you easily see how many visitors reach a certain page or perform a certain action and see where visitors may be losing interest along the way. You can use this information to make adjustments that optimize your site for conversion.

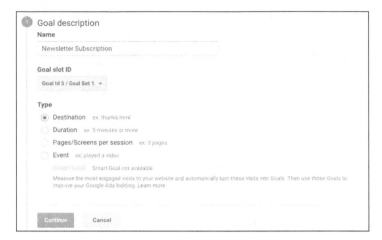

FIGURE 4-7:
Sample goals in
Google Analytics.

Google Analytics allows you to create four different types of goals, based on the specific interactions you may be interested in measuring; this list describes when to use them:

>> **Destination:** When you need to track a unique page or screen, like a thank you page, which more often than not indicates that the user has experienced, or is on their way to experiencing, value from your product.

>> **Event:** When you need to track specific actions and/or interactions with page elements where the URL doesn't change, like clicking a Play Podcast button or tapping on an ad.

>> **Duration:** When you need to track how long people spend on specific parts of your site, like the pricing page (and whether that time spent is necessary).

>> **Pages/screens per session:** When you need to track how many pages or screens people see on their way to experiencing value (or not).

After you've set up a goal, it can take anywhere from hours to days to start seeing data, depending on site traffic levels. Google Analytics reports on goal performance in the Overview section, under Conversions: Choose Conversions ⇨ Goals ⇨ Overview from the main menu. Then you can see the conversion rates of your goals and how they perform over time.

REMEMBER

You may need to measure more than key actions within Google Analytics. Other actions that supplement, or that are dependent on, these bigger actions need to be measured as well. For example, signing up for your email list may help people keep your brand foremost in mind when buying, but may have no immediate impact in terms of product usage or purchase. So, beyond your key actions, it's important to think through supporting secondary actions.

To reiterate, because Google Analytics is an aggregate analytics tool, it doesn't tell you who takes any particular action, but it does tell you how many times a certain action took place in a certain period.

Funnels

If goals are a measure of what people did, funnels tell you how they got to the place where they completed those actions. Identifying which step(s) people drop off on their way to a key action lets you come up with hypotheses for tests to mitigate those issues. Alternatively, if you see users skipping steps, that may tell you that the path to the key action may be longer than necessary.

Let's say you run an ecommerce site. A critical action would be to complete a purchase. The purchase funnel could be visualized this way:

Visit Product Page ⇨ Add Product to Cart ⇨ View Cart ⇨ Go to Payment Page ⇨ Complete Purchase

REMEMBER

Goal data (including the funnel) start working only after you create them. You can view your funnel data in the Funnel Visualization report, as shown in Figure 4-8: Choose Conversions ⇨ Goals ⇨ Funnel Visualization from the main menu.

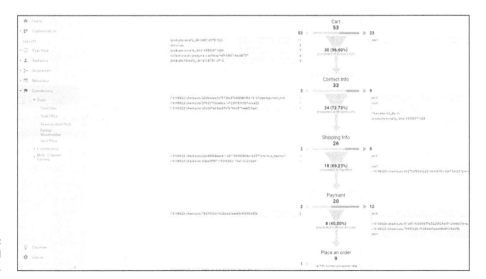

FIGURE 4-8: Sample funnel visualization.

You can set goals in terms of *events* — actions taken by a user — or by page views. "But," you might say, "what if my funnel has a mix of events and page views? In that case, can I not set events to measure the performance of my funnels?"

You can, but you need to get creative. For example, if you have a funnel where there's only way to reach the next screen (it's a strict, sequential process, in other words), you can make each step a goal. Yes, you have to visualize the funnel manually, but you will know how many people make it from one step to the next.

"But," you might also say, "funnels in real life are rarely straight lines." That is true. I discuss ways to account for real-world scenarios in Chapter 6.

TIP

It is beyond the scope of this book to go in depth into Google Analytics. Fortunately, Google itself has created an amazing — and free — resource with Google Analytics Academy. This site contains a series of courses to take you from beginner to power user in a systematic way. If you want to dive deeper into Google Analytics, I recommend Google Analytics Academy. It's free!

Understanding behavioral analytics

Aggregate user analytics tools provide you with overall data about how people who come to your site behave. This is great for getting a macro picture of how your business grows, but sometimes you need more than that, because such tools tend to tell you only *what* happened, but not *who* performed any action. Neither do aggregate user analytics tools extend beyond your website, so if you don't have a web-based product, you're seeing only a partial picture of the customer journey, and you're forming an incomplete understanding of how to grow your product. And, if your product is an app, aggregate user analytics tools won't help you much, either. Enter behavioral analytics.

Behavioral analytics show the actions that specific people take when using your product. They present these actions as a timeline that represents each customer's journey. They reveal new insights into the behavior of people using your product, helping you understand how your users act and why. This data allows you to make predictions about what they might do in the future. And, if you can reasonably predict how people might behave, you can then create optimal experiences for discrete user segments, which raise the odds of making your product more valuable to your customers.

Behavioral analytics tools show you what actions people take on a site or app over time, whether they're clicks, downloads, or anything else. This data can be viewed in aggregate, where people are grouped based on certain common characteristics, or individually. In either case, people remain identified, no matter how you slice the data.

With the help of behavioral analytics tools, your growth teams can answer more complicated questions about product usage, or lack thereof. Without such tools and the ability to identify who performed what actions, you'd be back to using anonymized aggregate data that wouldn't allow you to get to the heart of any problem areas.

The ability of behavioral analytics tools to provide granular usage information is based on uniting two factors: user identification and event tracking. It feeds the greatest power of behavioral analytics tools — which is the ability to segment users across various criteria and combine that with specific actions you're interested in tracking. This is what gives you a holistic view of the customer journey. You can then use this information to run tests to confirm hypotheses that lead to greater value being delivered to customers.

Behavioral analytics in action

When it comes to analytics tools, the bottom line is that you're now in a position to understand your customers at a much deeper level. Imagine that you were responsible for growing Amazon's book sales. You could decide to analyze a segment of users based on the number of reviews they read and the number of purchases made. This would make it easy to see the minimum number of reviews that most people read before they buy a book. This in turn would allow you to test displaying this minimum number of reviews by default and its impact on book sales.

You could take this analysis even further by answering questions like these:

>> Who buys books only when they're on sale?

>> Who prefers to buy books in-app versus on a website?

>> Who buys books mostly as gifts?

(And so on, to further customize people's experiences to ones they prefer.)

Lastly, by combining data from your acquisition campaigns with product usage data, you can begin to understand which marketing channels are the most profitable and then double-down on testing more ways to attract the kind of customers who will stick around longer and in turn derive more value from your product.

This gives you the foundation of a system that lets you answer key questions across the customer journey. Going back to the AARRR framework I discuss earlier in this chapter, in the section "Applying Pirate Metrics also known as AARRR)," you could answer queries like these:

>> **Acquisition:** Which channel is the most profitable?

>> **Activation:** Which actions do users who buy the product perform, and in what order?

>> **Retention:** What kinds of notifications lead to follow-up actions?

>> **Referral:** How many days should you wait before asking for a review in the app store?

>> **Revenue:** What common characteristics are shared by customers who upgrade?

TIP

There's a lot more involved in deciding between the implementation of behavioral analytics versus aggregate user analytics, so it can (and should) take longer to evaluate which one works best for your situation. This is primarily because, beyond inserting the necessary tracking code for the tool into your site or app, you also need developer resources to code events that you will use to track specific actions on an ongoing basis. You then need to evaluate how data is reported and how easy it is to stitch together data across all systems that house information about your customer's journey. You also have more choice with these tools, and you may have to use two or more such tools to form an even clearer picture of the customer journey.

REMEMBER

The best tools integrate with other tools so that you can generate comprehensive reports of how people behave and where your greatest growth opportunities may lie.

Popular behavioral analytics tools are Amplitude, Firebase, Flurry, Heap, Kissmetrics, and Mixpanel, among others. They all have free plans that will help you evaluate which core features address your needs. Whichever you pick, you need to ensure that they provide you with these ingredients:

- User and event data

- Different ways to query and visualize data

- The ability to easily create funnels and *cohort reports* — reports of groups of people that share similar attributes, like what channel they came from or the date they first visited

- Integrations with other data and business tools

- The ability to perform *A/B tests* — tests where different versions of the same product or site element are used in order to make comparisons

- Real-time access to data

Here are a few other considerations:

- Robust documentation

- The ability to create custom notifications

- Recommendations on next steps based on data

Implementing behavioral analytics with Amplitude

Amplitude is a behavioral analytics tool that makes it easy to understand user behavior as well as the impact of marketing decisions. I'm using Amplitude as an illustrative example for what you can expect to do when implementing a behavioral analytics tool simply because I've had firsthand experience with it.

Behavioral analytics needs planning to implement correctly. You can set yourself up for success by following these steps before implementing Amplitude:

1. **Create goals.**

   Just as you did with Google Analytics, create goals for key actions within your product and for any supporting secondary actions. This ensures that you're comparing the same elements when looking at similar trends in different tools.

2. **Create funnels.**

   Again, just as you created your ideal paths for people to get from one important step to another in Google Analytics, repeat that process here.

3. Create a tracking plan.

Now that you know the specific steps people will take, you need to track the key points to measure who is making it through those points and who isn't. Every aspect of your product that you choose to track is called an *event.*

You need to come up with a systematic way of naming these events because they can become complicated to keep track of as your product grows. Amplitude has helpfully provided detailed guidance and templates for naming events at https://help.amplitude.com/hc/en-us/articles/115000465251-Data-Taxonomy-Playbook.

WARNING

Show some restraint when you choose which events to measure. Just because you've created a funnel doesn't mean that you need to measure every part of it, at least to start off with. Keep it simple at first by picking a few key steps within your funnel that are important toward delivering value and the steps that tell you that value is being delivered.

If you try to track everything from the get-go, you'll overload yourself with too much data, making key insights harder to extract — not to mention that each event needs to be coded by your growth engineer as a snippet of JavaScript. Coding events for every step is time consuming and prevents you from getting on with the business of analyzing the customer journey and understanding where your greatest opportunities lie. Undoubtedly, as you analyze the customer journey, you'll identify other events that need tracking. The point is to understand what the results of tests are telling you about the need for more events so that you're always making progress and updating your tracking plan as you make such decisions.

4. Decide how to identify users.

This is one of the key reasons for using a behavioral analytics tool. Your product might have a web version and apps on iOS and Android. Without a behavioral analytics tool, it would be difficult — if not impossible — to stitch together the customer journey of any single user across platforms. So, however you decide to identify users within your product (using their email, for example, or another alphanumeric string of characters), that decision needs to be made before implementing the tool.

5. Implement Amplitude.

Now you can take steps to integrate Amplitude with your product via a software development kit (SDK) and/or an API, at which point you can then set up the method for assigning unique user IDs and key events in your tracking plan.

Unlike with Google Analytics, it gets a little bit technical from here on out and you will need engineering help to get your setup implemented correctly. Fortunately, Amplitude has amazing documentation that will guide you and your engineers every step of the way. You can find the documentation that covers the steps I summarized and technical details that I didn't get into here: `https://help.amplitude.com/hc/en-us/categories/200409887-Getting-Started`.

REMEMBER

Before going live, always test the implementation to ensure that events and users are being tracked correctly. After you've verified it, you can get on with the task of analyzing the customer journey.

TIP

You will likely need more tools than just the ones I've mentioned so far in this chapter as you get more proficient at extracting insights from tests. But having at least these foundational analytics tools will go a long way toward illuminating your performance. I do, however, provide some essential recommendations for tools to consider at the end of this chapter so that you have some context for the kinds of tools you may need.

Conducting a Growth Audit

Webster's Dictionary defines an *audit* as "a methodical examination and review." Though you typically hear of it in the context of taxes, in the growth context, the intent is much the same. A growth audit, then, is just an exploration of your current growth strategy undertaken in order to understand what you're doing and how you're doing it.

REMEMBER

The whole point of such an analysis should be to help identify how your business grows today and potential areas of opportunity (or trouble) in the future. It should allow you to "zoom out" and ask bigger questions about why you do the things you do and whether they're still the right things to continue doing. You may just find that conditions have changed since the initial setup — meaning that you no longer need to do things a certain way.

If you're familiar with the five interconnected phases known as Define, Measure, Analyze, Improve, and Control, or DMAIC, used as part of Lean Six Sigma initiatives, the intent of a growth audit is similar, where you analyze a specific process for waste and inefficiency and put in place mechanisms to improve it moving forward.

TIP

If you're the first growth hire, performing an audit is imperative to your success. It can take some time to get all the information you need, given how mature the data culture of your organization is. You may also need to spend time convincing key stakeholders, including your boss and even the CEO, about the importance of this activity on future growth.

REMEMBER

Growth requires buy-in at the highest levels, and generating support for this activity is as important as running weekly tests.

You want to learn three main outcomes as a result of this growth audit:

>> What's the current state of growth of the business?

>> What key numbers is the business measuring?

>> What is the business using to measure these numbers?

Assessing the current state of growth of the business

Think of this assessment like you would an annual health checkup. As part of this, you want to understand the answers to these questions:

>> **What is the North Star Metric (NSM), and what is its trend?**

You may find that the company you've joined hasn't identified this yet, and you may have to talk to the executive team to help them understand the importance of this metric and the need to define one.

As part of this assessment, you also need to investigate revenue growth. Logically, if you've picked the right NSM, you should see a correlation to revenue growth as well.

>> **What are the main forces behind its current trend?**

The cause(s) may be changes within acquisition channels or it may have something to do with the product, which is something you need to determine. You will have to start to gain a handle on the growth model for the business to understand the big picture of what the customer journey looks like and conversion rates at each stage.

Exploring key business measurements

As you answer the questions outlined in earlier sections of this chapter, you start to get a deeper look at the growth model and understand all the numbers the business believes to be important. This will be, by definition, a detailed look at the customer journey.

Retention rate, customer growth rate, and annual contract/order volumes should be among the key numbers you look at here, and they will all bear some correlation to your North Star Metric (NSM).

As you dig into the numbers, you will likely need to understand the history behind them as well. This will mean deeper conversations with key stakeholders to find out how they arrived at those numbers.

If the organization has a history of running tests, you'll also want to dig into past objectives and see which tests were run. These objectives and tests should map to hypotheses to grow numbers the business says it cares about. As a result, you'll also gain an appreciation for what the growth process — however informal — has been so far. You'll also learn about any existing challenges in executing the growth process, whether those are related to people resources or other matters.

Evaluating the tools that businesses use to measure their numbers

As a by-product of learning key numbers, you'll start to be able to answer questions about the *growth stack* of the company — all the tools used for growth-related activities across the customer journey, in other words.

You will of course learn about all the tools in use. But you should ask other questions, like these:

>> Are these tools integrated in some way to provide comprehensive reporting, or is reporting done on an individual basis?

>> Do the tools provide a complete picture of the customer journey, or are there gaps?

>> How much detail is in the data from each tool?

>> Can you trust the data?

>> Do you see any discrepancies?

Without asking questions like these, you will never know whether you have opportunities to influence the health of the data the company relies on. It helps to be systematic about this. Don't forget to document these questions and their answers in a central document so that you have a comprehensive view of your next steps.

More Context on Tools

For the most part, I've never been opinionated about which tools should be used for what purpose. I've had the mentality that if the tools I'm currently using are not giving me the answer I'm looking for, then I need to investigate adding another tool to the mix so that I can be smarter after analyzing my tests. The answer that I'm looking for can obviously change depending on the test, but it is generally the result of one of these questions:

>> **What happened?**

Quantitative analytics tools like Google Analytics and Amplitude that you've just read about provide this answer.

>> **Why did it happen?**

Qualitative tools like Hotjar and FullStory provide more context around the actions people are taking.

>> **How and When did it happen?**

Pretty much every testing tool like Google Optimize or Optimizely will give you details around conversions when you test different versions of the same product elements. Even tools that are not dedicated testing tools like Unbounce, which is a landing page builder, have the ability to test different versions of pages, putting them in this category of tool.

>> **Can I capture, share, or report on the learnings effectively?**

This category of tools relates to workflows and tools that improve the productivity or the efficiency of learning from data. Sometimes they're as simple as a shared Excel spreadsheet; other times it can be a programming tool you can use to create scripts that help you analyze groups of data faster and in some cases they're dashboards.

You may not have tools across all of these categories when you start, but you will eventually end up at a point where you need richer answers and you need to move faster. Knowing what questions you're being prevented from answering will help you identify what tools you may need.

Depending on the maturity of your company, you will have different priorities which will impact which questions are more critical to answer first.

When you're just past product-market fit, your biggest priority is likely to ensure that you understand how people get to the "aha moment" where people keep coming back to use your product. So your focus should be to ensure that you answer the "what happened" question as well as possible. You'll want to follow up on some of that data with "why did it happen" and only when you understand these two things — from a product perspective — can you start testing to build on those insights.

SEEING THE CUSTOMER JOURNEY AS A HERO'S JOURNEY

I find it useful to think of the customer lifecycle as a journey — specifically, a hero's journey. American professor and author Joseph Campbell popularized the idea of the hero's journey in his 1949 book *The Hero with a Thousand Faces*. He laid out the basic pattern of the journey this way:

> "A hero ventures forth from the world of common day into a region of supernatural wonder: fabulous forces are there encountered and a decisive victory is won: the hero comes back from this mysterious adventure with the power to bestow boons on his fellow man."

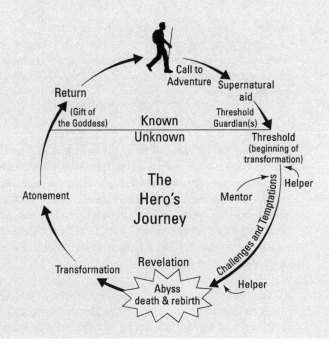

(continued)

(continued)

Countless stories, like *The Lord of the Rings, Star Wars,* and the *Harry Potter* series and beyond have used this construct. Dan Harmon, another American writer and TV producer, simplified Campbell's illustration into these eight steps:

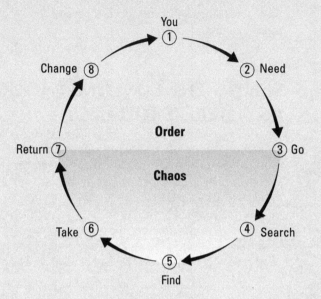

This model aligns perfectly with the idea of the North Star Metric (NSM) I discuss in Chapter 1. If you buy into the notion that the purpose of your business is to grow the amount of value you deliver to your customers, then, from a certain point of view, you're granting them special powers to achieve their goals. In other words, you're creating heroes.

When you're at a state where you've run tests on different product elements and have a good handle on the what, why, when, and how questions, your growth will start to become more predictable and sustainable. A hallmark of this is generally having the product experience nailed down and one solid acquisition channel that's working well. The priority now is to squeeze as much growth as possible out of that channel, which means a lot of testing to answer the "how and when" from a channel perspective. You may start to introduce some efficiencies now with tools that support that need.

As you grow beyond this point, you'll rinse and repeat this process for newer kinds of customers that will have shown up to nail down the product experience for them and also be testing newer channels to keep growth going strong.

IN THIS CHAPTER

» **Discovering how users find out about your product**

» **Defining the aha moment for your product**

» **Enticing users to come back and use your product**

» **Motivating users to pay for your product**

» **Inspiring users to talk about your product**

Chapter **5**

Diving into the Customer Journey

I f there's one concept you'll read about a lot in this book, it's that growth hacking is a process. I also hammer home the point about how sustainable growth happens when you increase the value you provide to your customers. You increase that value by looking for opportunities to increase value at every point in their interaction with your business. Thinking about that interaction, you'll soon notice many discrete opportunities to increase value, and you'll notice that such opportunities generally flow in a certain order. I'd argue that understanding this general order is crucial when it comes to orienting yourself toward the biggest opportunities to grow value. I talk more about specific customer journey frameworks in Chapter 4, but first I provide a macro view of the various touch points within the customer journey.

REMEMBER

These points of interaction within a customer journey start before someone has even experienced your product and extend to their being so happy with your product that they can't help but tell everyone they know how great your product is. I walk you through these stages and some considerations to think about at each one.

So, How Do Users Find Out about Your Product, Anyway?

Build it and they will not come. There's so much that already has people's attention and so many others trying to steal a slice of that attention that you simply cannot expect that people will magically find out about your product and start adopting it in droves. That means you have to find out where a lot of the people who want your product already are. This area is what marketing has traditionally been about: Make people aware of your product, get them excited about a certain promise, and then prime them to try it out.

Language fit

Finding folks where they are is important, but before you tackle that task, it's a good idea to look at the concept of language fit, one that I first heard about from James Currier, a former start-up founder himself and now an investor. If product-market fit is building something people want, *language fit* deals with how you communicate your product's value in a way that they understand it. Without this understanding, you can never tap into the potential of any marketing effort.

REMEMBER

Marketing your product is all about communicating what your company does and what your product does and how it can help people achieve their goals. It's a reflection of your future customers' psychology. It sets expectations. It follows then, that successful marketing is about eliciting a reaction from (more and more) people who resonate with that language, because the way you describe the problem and solution is how they would, too.

Imagine if Airbnb executives referred to their site as a "room renting marketplace." What does that even mean to the average person? But saying something like, "Book rooms in people's houses anywhere"? Now, that statement is easier to understand by people who are looking for alternatives to hotels. Or, what if YouTube had prioritized communicating "Upload your videos for free" versus "Broadcast yourself"? The point is that only after you understand language fit can you be successful at uncovering where more people who speak this language might be.

There's no big secret to discovering the right language. Just talk to people and ask them to describe, irrespective of the words you yourself have used initially, what they perceive as the value of your product in their own words. Record the words they use (on paper or actually record these sessions to transcribe later). After you've spoken to 20-30 such people, you may start to see patterns in the words people use. If you do, you might have found and initial group of people who all feel like your product meets a similar need. If not, keep talking to more people till you see a pattern emerge.

Different ways users can find you

The most common term for the places your customers and potential customers might be is to refer to them as *channels.* (Some folks say *acquisition channels* — it's the same thing.) Here are the two most common ways acquisition channels are characterized:

>> *Paid* **acquisition** refers mainly to ads, sponsorships, and so on, where the implication is that there's a monetary transaction for a certain amount of visitor traffic.

>> *Organic* **acquisition** refers to channels like content marketing, customer referrals, free PR, social media posts, and so on. The understanding here is that you have not paid a third party for this traffic; it's the result of activities your team has produced. In both cases, the activities can be online or offline.

To be honest, this distinction between paid and organic has never worked for me because no matter what kind of acquisition you do, it costs your business, whether it's in time or money and whether it's immediately or later. There really aren't any 100 percent unpaid acquisition channels.

So even though most marketing teams will use the paid and organic terminology to organize and communicate details of such campaigns, I like to categorize acquisition channels in two ways. First, who is doing more of the work to attract new customers — you or your existing users? Second, will activities within that channel have a generally predictable frequency, or are they likely to vary based on the need and opportunity?

This brings up the obvious question of what possible acquisition channels are even available to begin with?

Gabriel Weinberg and Justin Mares, the authors of *Traction: How Any Start-up Can Achieve Explosive Customer Growth*, identified these 19 possible ways to acquire users:

>> **Viral marketing:** You grow by encouraging your users to refer other users.

>> **Public relations (PR):** You get your name mentioned in traditional media outlets, like newspapers, magazines, and TV.

>> **Unconventional PR:** You do something unexpected, like publicity stunts or doing business in a way that no one else does, in order to draw media attention.

>> **Search engine marketing (SEM):** You advertise on search engines to consumers who are already looking to solve a particular problem.

- >> **Social Media and display ads:** You run ads on popular sites like YouTube or Facebook to reach new customers.

- >> **Offline ads:** You run ads on TV, radio, billboards, and infomercials and in newspapers and magazines, or you create flyers and other local advertisements.

- >> **Search engine optimization (SEO):** You ensure that your website shows up in key search results so that you can cheaply acquire lots of highly targeted traffic.

- >> **Content marketing:** You generate high-quality content that attracts outsized attention from people interested in a topic, which in turn drives traffic to the business.

- >> **Email marketing:** After you have a prospect's attention, you use email to convert, retain, and monetize them.

- >> **Engineering as marketing:** You build tools, calculators, or widgets that people can use for free for giving up contact information for you to nurture them into customers.

- >> **Targeting blogs:** You target niche blogs (or microinfluencers) to talk about your product to their highly engaged audiences.

- >> **Business development:** You partner up and create strategic relationships that produce a mutual benefit.

- >> **Sales:** You create sustainable and scalable processes to make it easier for customers to buy. This is mostly seen in the B2B world, where transactions can be complex.

- >> **Affiliate programs:** You enhance your distribution by allowing other people or companies to sell your product for a commission.

- >> **Existing platforms:** You piggyback off a huge platform like Facebook or an app store, leveraging the attention of that large user base toward your product.

- >> **Trade shows:** You showcase your product to a specific industry and, more importantly, to the decision-makers who attend such events.

- >> **Offline events:** You sponsor or host offline events — of any size — putting your product in front of a qualified audience in order to generate interest.

- >> **Speaking engagements:** You speak at high-profile events, which results in your product being promoted to an interested audience as a natural consequence of promoting you.

- >> **Community building:** You grow by forming passionate communities around your product.

WARNING

Each of these channels deserves its own book (and there are many). The larger issue to be aware of is that channels are always in flux. What works today won't work tomorrow.

A few years ago, James Currier, whom I mention earlier, published a graphic showing the evolution of channels to demonstrate this point. (See Figure 5-1.) It shows, for example, how Facebook as a channel wasn't even available until around 2006 because Facebook itself wasn't a thing before that. However, right around then, MySpace was a very popular thing that allowed you a way to reach a lot of people. If you follow just the MySpace and Facebook lines you'll see how their individual efficacy changed over time.

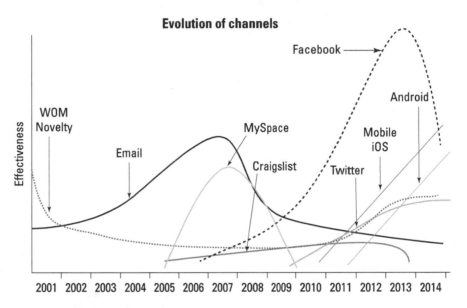

FIGURE 5-1:
Evolution of
channels.

This holds true today more than ever. And the frequency of change is only accelerating, among not only existing channels but also new channels constantly emerging. TikTok wasn't even popular when Currier drew the infographic shown in the figure more than 5 years ago, just as an example. But at the time this book was published, you already had marketers experimenting with TikTok to figure out its potential.

What this means is that any book or post written about an acquisition channel will likely be at least partially obsolete by the time it's published. This, if anything, should drive home the point that when it comes to acquisition, no one will ever know everything about it forever. There's just too much happening within one channel, let alone all of them, for anyone to be an expert in everything. Therefore, the need to experiment within channels that are working and channels that could work for you tomorrow is an ongoing effort for your product.

Categorizing channels

If you organize the 19 acquisition channels that are out there by who is doing most of the work that gets more people to your product — you or your current customers — as well as by relative frequency, you see something like the chart shown in Table 5-1. (Your categorization may look slightly different, based on your specific situation.)

TABLE 5-1

Channels Categorized by Who Does Most of the Work

You (Predictable Frequency)	You (Variable Frequency)	Your Customers or Others (Unpredictable Frequency)
Search engine marketing	Public relations (PR)	Viral marketing
Social Media and display ads	Unconventional PR	Affiliate programs
Search engine optimization	Offline ads	Existing platforms
Content marketing	Engineering as marketing	Community
Email marketing	Targeting blogs	
Sales	Business development	
	Trade shows	
	Offline events	
	Speaking engagements	

I categorize acquisition channels this way because it helps me understand, at a high level, where to focus my energies. If I know that one channel is dependent on opportunities that show up on their own schedule (for example, speaking engagements) and one is just going to part of your marketing channel mix, no matter what (for example, advertising), that tells me about how to prioritize my efforts — how much time and effort I might have to dedicate to that channel at any time, in other words. It even tells me that if some channels inherently vary in terms of my ability to rely on them, that variability applies to how soon I might see results as well. Finally, if success with some channels is more a function of customers or others doing more of the work, then I know that dependency exists within the product or other resources I might have to provide, which then tells me about time and cost needed.

TIP

When I'm starting out, I try to test within one channel from each of the categories shown in Table 5-1 to help me understand more about which channel has the biggest potential. As I gather more information, I swap out channels from other categories to find the other winners.

As you're reading this section, you may wonder, "How do I know which channels to pick, whether I'm starting out or trying to find new channels to go after?" That's what the next section is all about.

Prioritizing channels to test

You may be tempted to first go after what seems easier to do or channels that are seemingly cost-free, but there's nothing systematic about that, and you'll likely waste time doing it this way.

Brian Balfour, the CEO of Reforge (and former VP of growth at HubSpot), came up with a methodology I've used a lot in order to pick which channels to go after first (or next). He proposed a prioritization matrix that has these variables:

>> **Cost:** Estimates of how much it will cost to run tests to acquire users in a channel

>> **Targeting:** The ease with which you can reach your best audience and other audiences

>> **Input time:** An estimate of how much time it would take to prepare and launch a small test to see how this channel performs

>> **Output time:** An estimate of how much time it would take to start seeing the results of your experiments

>> **Control:** The ease and ability to make changes after the experiment is live — or even shut down the test, if you need to

>> **Scale:** An estimate of how much of your intended market you can reach by using a channel

Each of these variables is an aspect of acquisition that you need to test and learn about in order to understand where your biggest opportunities may lie in a given channel.

To avoid getting bogged down in the details, Balfour proposed a simple Low, Medium, or High rating for each of these variables for a given channel. Depending on your product, the scores for these variables for any channel will naturally vary. Here you can use what you're now able to infer about each channel from the categorization I mention earlier, in the section "Categorizing channels," to inform these ratings.

If you combine Balfour's matrixed approach with the specificity of the 19 acquisition channels summarized by Weinberg and Mares, you get a grid that looks like Figure 5-2:

	Cost	Targeting	Control	Input Time	Output Time	Scale
Perfect World	Low	High	High	Low	Low	High
Viral Marketing						
Public Relations (PR)						
Unconventional PR						
Search Engine Marketing						
Social and Display Ads						
Offline Ads						
Search Engine Optimization						
Content Marketing						
Email Marketing						
Engineering as Marketing						
Targeting Blogs						
Partnerships/ Biz Dev						
Sales						
Affiliate Programs						
Existing Platforms						
Trade Shows						
Offline Events						
Speaking Engagements						
Community						

FIGURE 5-2: A channel prioritization matrix, combining Balfour and Weinberg/Mares' work.

You can use this grid to undertake the exercise of assigning Low/Medium/High ratings for each channel now. As you undertake this exercise, you'll find that some scores are easier to calculate than others (even with minimal data at your disposal) because, no matter what your product is, some universal truths pertain to all products. For example, ads have High control. Speaking engagements do not. Output time for community is Low, and so on. Fill out those obvious slots for your situation across all channels first, and then do the rest.

You can repurpose the ICE scoring framework I talk about in Chapter 8 to assign scores from 1–10 to each of these variables and then use the average score for each channel to initially determine priority. In that case, you just add a column, Average Score, to the end of the grid.

In the ideal scenario, you'd have a channel like this one:

Cost: Low

Targeting: High

Control: High

Input Time: Low

Output Time: Low

Scale: High

Sadly, this scenario rarely happens. That means you need to prioritize based on your individual situation. This is where hypotheses come into play. Depending on what you're trying to learn — is it all about cost? targeting ability? scale? — you need to treat that variable as the most important factor and then see how close the other variables come to meeting the ideal channel scenario. Finally, you start testing for that specific hypothesis.

The most common scenario is that you'll be constrained most by budget, so sort your table by channels that are low cost, and then see how closely the remaining variables reach the ideal scenario channel, based on what you're trying to learn.

You now have a systematic approach to learn more about how users find out about your product.

Seeing What Excites Your Customers

As of this writing, over 3 billion people are on the Internet globally. The number of products and services being built to meet the needs of these people is growing every day as well. This makes it harder not only for your product to stand out but also for you to maintain people's interest in it. In many cases, people may hear about a product, come check it out, and then leave. This scenario is more common than most people realize.

To give you a sense of how common this scenario is, a study in 2018 by mobile intelligence start-up Quettra found that most apps in the Google Play Store lose almost 80 percent of their users within three days of download.

REMEMBER

Acquiring users is meaningless if you suffer from "leaky bucket syndrome," where most of the people who show up end up leaving. Sustainable growth for your product — and, ultimately, your business — depends on people sticking around, because, if they stick around, they do so only because your product provides value.

If you were to look only at your own analytics and then at the ratio of people who show up versus those who take any meaningful action (signing up for a product, buying a product, participating in a free trial, and so on), you'll find that number to be depressingly small. This is just reality. Before you start getting overly depressed, though, know that even the best products don't retain 100 percent of their users.

So what factors can you look at to determine users will stick around after you've done the hard work of acquiring users, makes them stick around? It starts with understanding the importance of activation to growth.

Activation is a fancy way to describe the action(s) that contributes to your future customers understanding the value of your product and taking the next step with it to meet their goals. What's important to understand is that, irrespective of the type of product involved, users will take an action, or a sequence of actions, with your product that tells you they have an initial level of resonance with your product's value and are open to trying it out. This is the figurative light bulb in people's heads lighting up as they go "aha!" It's when people have an emotional reaction that tells them there's something your product can do that other products can't do or can't do better.

Here are some examples of activation metrics capable of quantifying those "aha" moments that have been publicly mentioned or documented by people on early teams of some popular products:

>> **Facebook:** Connect with seven friends in ten days.

>> **Twitter:** Follow 30 users.

>> **Slack:** Send 2,000 messages between team members.

>> **Pinterest:** Post weekly pins (at least 1 or more), four weeks after sign-up.

>> **Dropbox:** Save a single file in a folder on a single device.

With all of these examples, odds were very high that if someone performed these actions, they would continue to use the products.

REMEMBER

Depending on your product, it may take people multiple experiences before they finally understand it's value. This is especially true of complex products that need careful consideration, like ones that need a demo or another form of guided discovery. Physical products are even more complicated, where people can't interact or try them out online. So it's not a hard-and-fast rule that the light bulb will go off on the first encounter. The goal, however, is for each interaction to move people closer to realizing that your product is the best one that meets their needs.

REMEMBER

As you learn more about your users or as your product changes, you may find that the aha moment may be different based on why any person decided to try your product. The reason someone may do so is closely connected to their intent, which leads to how they found out about your product. That in turn should inform how they experience its value.

Onboarding versus Activation

You'll occasionally come across folks who use *onboarding* and *activation* interchangeably. That's flat-out wrong. I didn't distinguish between the two terms either, until I read a discussion a few years back that Josh Elman (who is a VC now but was on the early team at Twitter) contributed to on GrowthHackers.

He described *onboarding* as a process that starts the first time someone hears of your product and continues until they're using it habitually. The part of this process where you come to the product and try it is when you start the activation process. This is the moment where the product teaches the users what it's all about and how it can help them achieve their goals. For products where users cannot form a habit immediately (which is true of most products), the steps of drawing users back and engaging them are the key to onboarding. After that, you have a user as either a *retained* user (I talk more about this topic in the later section "Get user feedback") or one that you've lost. If it's the latter case, you need to think of something else to restart the onboarding process.

REMEMBER

Onboarding begins at the point where you have the maximum possible level of attention from a potential user. That point can be within an acquisition channel or elsewhere within the product experience.

Morgan Brown, who was on the early GrowthHackers team, used Josh's explanation to come up with a rubric where it took answering only three questions to understand the interplay of onboarding and activation:

>> At what point are new users most engaged and paying the most attention to the product?

>> At that moment, what do you want them to know, feel, and do?

>> Does this moment equate to a must-have experience?

Here's a question I like to tack on to these:

>> What is the frequency with which a user is expected to experience value?

So, how do you get the answers to these questions to understand where aha moments exist? The next couple of sections spell out a useful strategy.

Use your own data first

The first, and most obvious, question to ask is how the experiences of those people who experienced an aha moment differ from those who didn't? Was there a behavioral pattern that was obvious from your analytics into what actions they took? If you were to create a list of 10 to 20 actions, or combinations of actions, associated with those people who continued to use your product, what patterns emerge for you?

Now, what happens when you exclude from that list any behaviors that were also taken by people who stopped using your product after a period that represents the most common point that people stop using your product? If you were to visualize what this looks like at a high-level, you'd get something like the Venn diagram in Figure 5-3

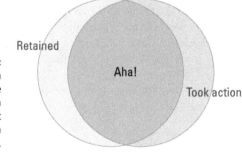

FIGURE 5-3: Actions taken by most people who retain within your product best are likely aha moments.

Such an investigation doesn't necessarily give you the complete answer, but it puts you on the right track.

A quick way to get started with the exercise is to first build a hypothesis for these items:

>> The expected frequency of value delivery (daily, weekly, monthly, quarterly, or annually)

>> The key step(s) signifying that the aha moment has been reached

>> The key step(s) predicting that those who have had their aha moment will stick around

Looked at mathematically, activation can be described this way:

> People who are still doing [value delivery actions] at [expected frequency] at or after [time period post-sign-up]

After collecting the required information, create a table for the frequency of each key action you're investigating, and try to find the percentage of overlap between these three elements:

>> Everyone who was retained

>> Everyone who performed an action

>> Everyone who performed that action within a certain period

The frequency that has the greatest percentage overlap gets you close to identifying the aha moment(s). (Table 5-2 gives you an idea of what I'm talking about.)

TABLE 5-2 **Calculating the Greatest Percentage Overlap for Key Action Frequency to Find an Aha Moment**

[Action Name] and Minimum Number of Occurrences	Number of Users Who Retained and Performed an Action n Times	Number of Users Who Retained and Did Not Perform an Action n Times	Total Number of Users Who Performed an Action n Times	Percentage Overlap between Column 2 and Column 4
1				
2				
3				
4				
5				
6				
7				
8				
9				
10				

Get user feedback

After you have formulated a hypothesis using your quantitative data, gather some qualitative feedback from your best users to add to your understanding of the aha moment. Conversations with your best retained users tells you more about why and how they experienced value the first time. This in turn gives you a more nuanced understanding of the language you need in order to communicate the core value of your product to a specific set of people.

This exercise can be as easy as sending a personal email to your best users or customers asking them for a 10-minute conversation by phone or video call to discuss their product experience — and relate what excited them about your product — so that you can create a great experience for everyone else. If you aren't getting a strong enough response, consider incentivizing them with a discount or a product upgrade — after all, these are your best users.

Repeat this same exercise with people who didn't stick around or buy (assuming that you have their contact information). Adjust your pitch to focus more on learning why the product wasn't a fit for them, though you'll get as much value out of learning from those who *didn't* experience value from your product. Much of your learning will end up revolving around why they ended up not being the right audience for your product (in which case you learn more about how to target the right people) or figuring out what stood in the way of their experiencing that value. If it's the latter case, you can address the issue quickly within your product with tests to raise the odds of people experiencing an aha moment and sticking around.

TIP

Be prepared for the fact that people who don't like your product may not be thrilled about receiving a call from you. You may need to incentivize with an Amazon gift card or similar item. The alternative is to use single-question exit surveys on the site when someone is about to leave without completing the steps that will lead to their aha moment. The question can be as simple as this:

> "What prevented you from trying, signing up for, or performing the core action(s) today?"

Then you can refine from there. (Tools like Hotjar or Qualaroo can be a big help in creating such surveys.)

If you can figure out the aha moment, that makes it easier to solve for the next task, which is retention.

Landing That Repeat Customer

Traditional marketing has rarely treated retention with the importance it deserves. After all, isn't it sexier to say, "We have 1,000 new leads" or "We have 10,000 new users"? Acquisition numbers are normally higher than retention numbers — not to mention the fact that once you have an activated user, your acquisition task is done. Retention, on the other hand, must slog to keep these users — a much harder task.

REMEMBER

Retention is at the core of growth hacking and, with all the attention that has come to growth, the importance of retention has never been more at the forefront. If you have good retention, you have users who keep paying you, and users who are paying you are more likely to be happy and willing to recommend you to others, which in turn feeds the acquisition bucket — and round and round we go.

You can think of retention as the mechanism by which you build the habit for your product with more people. If you have a software product, this means figuring out ways to reduce *churn* — the number of people who stop using your product. If you're an e-commerce solution, this means trying to understand what it takes to turn someone into a repeat purchaser, and so on. In many ways, this is an extension of the activation exercise.

Where do you start?

First, remember that if you have an activation issue or haven't figured out what activation even is for your product, you shouldn't be tackling issues that will build a habit for your product. In fact, you could consider activation as the first step of retention (because it is). Many people describe *activation* as short-term retention. This make sense because, without short-term retention, there's no long-term retention. The only reason to think of activation separately from a customer journey perspective is that it does have a discrete, quantifiable set of steps that set the stage for what happens next.

With that discussion out of the way, perhaps the best way to start is to ask the most basic question: What's the retention rate right now?

To begin to answer this question, you first need to know the frequency of usage for your product, which is a calculation you've already figured out when you understand your activation metrics.

Then it helps to go back and look at acquisition and divide your users into groups or cohorts. When dealing with retention, cohort analysis is integral, and tools like Amplitude, Mixpanel, and Heap have made this easy to figure out. Whichever tool you use, you'll ask the same questions of the tool to glean your retention insights.

REMEMBER

Cohorts are usually grouped by day or week or month of sign-up, but you can also create them by other characteristics, such as sign-up source or device type or another attribute. This allows you to see whether certain user characteristics are highly correlated with retention, which in turn helps make your acquisition activities and tests more focused.

Here are two big questions you're looking to answer via cohort analysis:

>> What channel do my most retained users come from?

>> What do these users have in common?

Armed with a sense of the retention rate of your most retained users, the next obvious question you need answered is this: What is it about the product experience that makes them come back? And, more importantly, why?

So, here you're looking to answer questions like these:

>> What features are making the product "sticky"?

>> Are any features making the product "unsticky"?

>> Why do people who take certain actions retain at a higher rate?

You then look from the other side of the puzzle to find out why people are leaving after they've become activated, a process known as mitigating churn or fighting churn. Here are the questions you're trying to answer:

>> What are the best ways to remind users to keep engaging with — and deriving value from — your product? Is it via email? Push notifications? SMS? Another method?

>> Are there any best times to notify users based on when it appears that they've stopped using the product?

>> What patterns can you observe about users stopping their usage?

If you're further along your journey and you have already addressed these issues, you're looking at impacting longer-term retention and keeping the spark alive (much like being in a long-term relationship with someone). These are the kinds of questions you're asking here:

>> Is ongoing engagement among existing users correlated with any features? If you in fact added features at the request of users, are users more engaged now?

>> Is any drop in engagement among existing users due to new features or any other activities?

>> Is new-user activation or retention impacted by any features you might have built for existing users?

REMEMBER

You can learn about how to retain users in many ways. The better you understand your retention numbers, the better you can communicate the value of your product, not only externally but also to the internal team, to be able to focus them more on what matters.

Inspiring Users to Pull Out Their Wallets

Pricing is such a complicated and hotly debated topic that few people can say with any honesty that they have a handle on it. First and foremost, it's not just about costs — it's about value and sometimes even perceived value (Exhibit A: Apple products versus those produced by Microsoft). I'm the first to admit I'm still learning more about it. (If it were my full-time job to understand pricing, I might have a better handle on it.) I'm guessing that unless you're an economist or you have years of experience with buying and selling something, you don't quite understand pricing completely, either.

The bottom line is that if you want to have a viable business, you have to charge for your product at some point. The one thing I absolutely do know is that everything you do should be guided by your NSM. So pricing should somehow be related to this topic as well.

It's safe to say, then, that whatever you decide to charge is aligned with the value your product provides and can potentially grow as your customers' needs (and the value they receive from your product) grow as well.

This is where the retention analysis you've done, about who your best-retained users are and which features drive the most long-term retention, can help you. If you were to find a feature that people keep using whether they're a new user or an existing one, this is where the value of your product is being felt the most. So, testing different prices based on usage of that feature might be a valid pricing strategy. The risk here is that you might go overboard and set a price that feels larger than the value being derived. If that's the case, you'll soon discover the error of your ways, quantitatively with the help of pricing tests and qualitatively by way of conversations and surveys with users.

Don't hesitate to talk about pricing with your users because you believe that there's a risk they may feel that the product isn't worth the they're paying for it. If that happens, you likely have more work to do to better communicate its value and then have those conversations again.

Patrick Campbell, CEO of Profitwell, a subscription software provider that also provides a set of useful financial metrics, suggests that you ask every applicable customer segment the following four questions in order to glean better insights about your pricing strategy:

>> At what point is the product so expensive that you'd never consider purchasing it?

>> At what point is the product becoming expensive, but you'd still consider purchasing it?

>> At what point is the product a great deal?

>> At what point is the product so cheap that you'd question its quality?

I'd call the Campbell model *value-based* pricing, and I feel that it's a great approach, but keep in mind that it's not the only way to price products. Two other approaches also have their adherents:

>> **Competitive-based pricing:** The idea here is to just copy your competitors pricing blindly, plus or minus a few percent. It's an easy way to get started with pricing if you don't know where to begin, but you absolutely must supplement that system with additional research to understand whether you're leaving money on the table and how you can differentiate yourself to allow raising prices in the future. Getting caught in a price war and having your product be thought of as just another commodity seriously impedes your ability to rely on pricing as a lever of growth for business.

>> **Cost-plus pricing:** Here's a simple idea — sell something for more than it costs to make it (including production costs, salaries, and so on) for a price that doesn't feel too egregious. It doesn't necessarily take into consideration any external factors, such as competitor pricing, pricing research, or value added to users. It's simply a reflection of the value you feel you add by making this new product. And although it's simple to implement, the fact that it's dissociated from the NSM makes it not something you want to do, or do for very long, if you're forced to go down this path for some reason.

What should become apparent is that, as with everything in growth, figuring out pricing is a process, too. It's never one-and-done.

Turning Product Users into Product Proselytizers

If you have happy users who derive value from your product, they should have no problem telling everyone they know about how great your product is and why everybody else should try it as well. The benefits of this action are obvious, because getting people to talk about your product with others is like getting free advertising. This means that the amount of money you pay to acquire new users decreases dramatically (and, in some cases, maybe even drop to zero). Word of mouth increases, brand awareness increases, and cost of acquisition decreases. (It's like the Holy Grail!)

Because the people doing the referring are most likely customers who are regular users of your product, the way they talk about your product will likely resonate with others like them. (There's that language fit again.) So referrals should not only help bring in more customers but also bring in more of the right customers, which makes retention easier for you.

In this day and age, people trust firsthand recommendations more than ever. People also recommend products or services they've found useful, because it makes them look knowledgeable to their audience, giving them some social capital that they've never had.

Your job, over time, is to make this into a repeatable process where your users or customers are rewarded for helping spread the word about your product. The easiest way to do this is by incentivizing someone to take that extra step and refer you — even when they love you — because this this has a "cherry on top" feeling to it.

The trick to making this step work is that what people receive for making the referral must match the means of deriving value from the product.

The best, and most often quoted, example of this process is probably Dropbox, whose referral program offered free storage space for every person you referred who joined the service.

Dropbox did something else that not many people had done before but that almost everyone else does now — offer a double-sided referral program. This twist made it so that you received a benefit and the person doing the referring received one as well. In this case, both of you received extra online storage space. Storage space was carefully selected because the Dropbox NSM revolves around access to your files on any device anywhere. Without the space to store all your files, you likely wouldn't use them for long.

This is why retailers, food delivery services, ride share services, subscription services, or anywhere else that you have to exchange money for value all have double-sided referral programs that give both the referrer and the referee money or a discount toward a future purchase.

It's not always the case that the referrer and the referee should receive the same reward. Much depends on the frequency of your usage. Say you run an e-commerce store for coffee mugs. It's not like people buy mugs every month. So, offering the referrer a discount for a future purchase that they may or may not make isn't a strong enough incentive (even though a discount for the referee's first purchase may be so). In this case, straight-up cash, or a gift card loaded with cash, might be just the right incentive for them to spread the word for you, especially if they can earn unlimited amounts in referrals and spend that money however they please (rather than be tied to spending that money at your store).

With the bare bones of a referral program in place, you can then start to make your referral process systematic by leveraging the insights gained about retention to inform how, how much, and at what frequency to communicate about your referral program. Just keep in mind that that you'll need to continue to test across these dimensions to look for further opportunities.

Not all referral programs go viral the way Dropbox's did. You don't hear about Doordash's referral program or Lyft's. Yet they all have this type of program because it works well enough to be a significant part of how they grow. And because the referral program plays a meaningful part in their growth, they invest time and effort in optimizing it.

If you take this systematic approach across every stage of your customer journey, you will have a far better understanding of your customers' motivations and be much better positioned to build a product that delivers value to them at every step of their journey with you.

3

Applying the Growth Hacking Process

IN THIS PART . . .

Following your North Star Metric

Analyzing product growth

Looking at growth opportunities

Carrying out (the right) tests

Establishing routines

Building a culture of sharing

Chapter **6**

Laying the Foundation for Growth

As with anything meant to be long-lasting, when it comes to setting in motion an engine of sustainable growth, you first need to create a strong foundation for that engine. With that foundation in place, you can put yourself in a position to execute a process that has been proven to work at some of the fastest growing companies around. After all, growth hacking is nothing if not methodical when it comes to exploring and acting on potential opportunities for breakout growth.

Doing It Like a Scientist: Developing and Testing Hypotheses

When you were in high school, you likely found yourself in science lab, where during the course of the year you ran a number of experiments. Whether it was physics, chemistry, or biology, you had to document your experiment plan in a certain format. That document probably had a structure like this:

» **Title:** A short description of the experiment

» **Hypothesis:** A short summary of the purpose of the experiment

>> **References:** Facts or data from external sources that justify the experiment

>> **Materials:** The list of items you needed to perform the experiment

   Ideally, this information would be detailed enough for someone else to repeat the experiment.

>> **Procedure:** A description of the actual steps you performed

>> **Expected Results:** A prediction of the range within which the experiment was supposed to provide results, with measurement units

>> **Observations and Data:** The data you obtained, including any tables and graphs

>> **Results:** The actual results of your experiment after you performed final calculations

>> **Conclusion:** A final statement of whether the experiment proved the hypothesis, possibly including next steps or other experiments for further study

Running a growth experiment is no different from this; it's just the context that's different. In school, it was in a lab. With growth hacking, it's happening within a customer journey.

REMEMBER

Many people overcomplicate growth hacking by thinking of it as a new methodology that you somehow need to master. The fact of the matter is, you already know the basic process (even if you need a refresher on the structure of an experiment plan). The age-old scientific method, where you identify a problem, gather data, formulate a hypothesis, and then test that hypothesis is at the heart of understanding how to grow your product.

At GrowthHackers, Sean Ellis always said that the best growth hack was to run more experiments. He used the phrase *high-tempo testing*. The more tests you ran, the faster your ability to learn about what worked and what didn't when it came to growing your product. This not only made you smarter about where opportunities for growth might come from but also provided a focus for future tests.

If you can grasp the idea that growth hacking is a systematic process, you are already ahead of most people trying to wrap their brains around this concept. It helps you avoid all the confusion that comes with the nonstop deluge of "growth hacking tips" you see every day.

Identifying Your North Star Metric

A common question that business leaders get asked is, "Why does your product exist?" The answer never is to make money. (Well, of course, you want to make money, but more on this in a bit.) The correct answer follows this format: "To help people do or accomplish something." That something is obviously different based on what your product does, but the central truth is that people use only things that add value to their lives.

A North Star Metric (NSM) is a number that helps you quantify the core value your product provides your customers. It follows, then, that if you grow the value your product provides, by definition your business will grow as well. This means that there has to be alignment between what your product does and what problem your customers want to solve. It also means that, by solving this problem, your business will make money.

REMEMBER

The purpose of your NSM is focus. But trying to grow this number is futile without first understanding your customers' motivations and what specific value they hope to get out of using your product. These qualitative insights will help drive the kind of product development that delivers on the promise your customers hope for, which in turn will impact your key metrics and lead to business growth.

WARNING

I've occasionally read articles and heard conversations that interchangeably use the idea of One Metric That Matters (OMTM) and the North Star Metric. (OMTM is described in great detail by Alistair Croll and Benjamin Yoskowitz in their book, *Lean Analytics*.) A closer read will inform you of one small (yet important) difference: The OMTM refers to the most important metric that matters for your business right now. This is because, at any point in time, the biggest opportunity (or problem) in front of you can, and will, keep changing. Your awareness of these opportunities and/or problems shapes what you focus on right now, making it your OMTM. In other words, your OMTM is analogous to objectives, which I cover in greater detail in Chapter 7.

By contrast, your NSM, like the North Star from which it takes its name, is unchanging. The NSM is what lights and guides your path, however you get there. This is not to say that your NSM might not need refocusing if evidence points to its being incorrect or misaligned. The difference is that the OMTM has a shorter-term utility and your NSM is meant for the long run.

Identifying your NSM provides a couple of giant benefits. First, it helps everyone in the company identify what they're all working toward, in a simple way (growing value to the customer, in other words). By definition, it also communicates that such growth is everyone's responsibility. As a consequence, it also helps everyone coordinate what they need to do every day to grow this value. The power of this metric in removing artificial barriers between groups cannot be under-stated, because this number moves beyond internal departmental metrics and revenue to a single, external one — one that is all about the customer and is devoid of politics or internal competition. Without such a number, it becomes a challenge to get the entire company to align around a common goal.

Secondly, the trajectory of the growth of your NSM becomes a clear indicator of how well you're doing with meeting your customer's needs over time. Based on the trend, it helps your company rally around appropriate initiatives to keep that trend moving in the right direction.

Revenue is not a North Star Metric

When I ask someone what their product's NSM is, the most common answer I get is "revenue." This puts the cart before the horse, because revenue is a result of delivering value, not the other way around. So, by definition, revenue is a *lagging* indicator of the health of the business. What you want is a *leading* indicator. Also — let's face it — just because you paid for something doesn't mean you got value from it.

The bigger problem with using revenue as an NSM is that it's an internal metric and growing this number without prioritizing the customer's needs can some-times get us to do things in order to impact revenue numbers without growing value. You *always* want your revenue strategy to be closely linked to how you deliver value.

Figuring out your product's North Star Metric

I tell anyone who'll listen that a product's NSM should align with how people derive value from it. When it comes down to it, you can provide value in only a few ways: You either increase something people want or decrease something they don't want. (Ideally you'd do both, but that's easier said than done.) When you give people more of what they want out of your product, you increase the desire for the value it provides them. Similarly, when you decrease what they don't want to deal with, you remove the friction, or difficulty with experiencing the value of your product.

I'm intentionally using the words "desire" and "friction" here because this allows me to co-opt another concept from Sean Ellis that he talks about in the context of conversions. He had a simple equation for conversion rate optimization that said: Desire – Friction = Conversion Rate. Applied to the context of an NSM, your prod-uct can either increase desire for something — causing you to increase the amount of time (and maybe even money) you're willing to spend on or with it — or reduce friction or difficulty by saving you time and/or money, providing value as a consequence.

A few examples might help illustrate what's what with this whole Desire/Friction dynamic:

» **Uber:** Uber's value is to reduce the unpredictability associated with trying to find an available taxicab. (Fun fact: Uber was initially called UberCab). So its NSM is the number of rides taken. If people take more rides, it follows that they're getting value from it. This NSM also works for the drivers, because, as more people want to use Uber to hail rides, it becomes more attractive for more drivers to be on the platform to earn money from those rides.

» **Facebook:** Facebook's value lies in providing you with an online feed of information about your friends, family, and topics you might be interested in. The more relevant it makes this feed, the more time you spend engaging with it. So Facebook tries to increase your desire for the content you engage with, which means you spend more time on Facebook doing certain things, like uploading pictures or liking and commenting on other people's updates. Facebook also keeps suggesting people or topics to engage with so that, no matter what, you have opportunities to engage with something every day. So, Facebook's NSM is the number of daily active users.

As you engage on Facebook, the company learns more about you and your preferences. This is turn allows it to monetize your behavior by serving you ads on the platform that advertisers can granularly target to specific characteristics about you.

Facebook is an example of an NSM that has evolved over time. Ed Baker, Facebook's first head of international growth, shared in an interview with Sean Ellis at the 2018 GrowthHackers conference that the company's first NSM was the number of weekly active users, where *active* meant that people engaged with an activity feed in certain ways that kept them engaged. Over time, engagement was found to be so high that they had to evolve it to the number of daily active users. The definition of *active* didn't change (much), but they had to adjust to the reality of the increased frequency of usage. Baker even predicted the NSM to evolve again soon, to the number of hourly active users.

» **Walmart:** Walmart's entire premise is about wide choice and savings. The company reduces friction in your life by saving you the time spent shopping at multiple stores while also helping you spend less on items you need. If it continues to provide that value, there's no reason for you to not keep buying from the store. So, Walmart's NSM might reasonably be the number of purchases completed.

Variations and exceptions to the rule

When it comes to exceptions to the rule, Amazon is an interesting example to consider. When it first started, all Amazon did was sell books. Its value lay in a) saving you the time of having to go to the bookstore and b) selling you books at a cheaper price. It reduced friction with the book buying process. So, its NSM would have been the number of orders delivered. It didn't matter how many books were in each order, but if more people ordered more books, that was a reflection of the value it provided.

This NSM worked well, even when it started selling other items. Amazon doesn't care as much about what you order or how much is in each order, as long as you keep ordering from it. It means much more to the company for you to be a repeat customer versus someone who spends a lot of money just once.

TIP

The NSM of number of orders delivered could apply to any e-commerce business.

The situation became interesting when Amazon added other distinct product lines, like Amazon Web Services (AWS). In this situation, it makes no sense for Amazon's NSM to be the number of orders. AWS provides on-demand cloud computing, which has a completely different value proposition — reducing the cost and effort of maintaining server infrastructure. This is where it makes sense that distinct product lines within a company have their own NSM, because the way to grow the value delivered will be markedly different for each product line.

When the final value delivery is online but outside your product

Another exception to consider is a product like Kayak, which, among other things, is an airfare aggregator. You can search for fares on its site and then click through to the airline site to complete the transaction. So, the final value — buying a ticket — is not delivered by Kayak.

In such instances, you have to look for a reasonable proxy action for your NSM. Kayak's value lies in reducing the time you spend visiting multiple sites to compare fares — reducing friction, in other words. Kayak does this by providing a nearly comprehensive listing of fares across airlines that allows you to make a comparison faster than you otherwise might and then click through to buy your ticket. This final act of clicking through to an airline site wouldn't happen if those airfare search results weren't useful. So, Kayak's NSM would be "the number of click-throughs," because the expectation would be that if you're clicking through to the airline site, you're likely ready to buy your ticket.

REMEMBER

I make a big deal about the fact that revenue isn't a great choice when it comes to your NSM. However, *recurring revenue* can be your NSM when you have a subscription business for a physical product. Consider a business like Barkbox, which delivers dog toys and treats monthly. Barkbox's value proposition is to save you time (and perhaps even money) finding high-quality items (some of which you may not even come across) and sends to your door. It's logical to say that you wouldn't continue your monthly subscription unless you thought that your dog *really* liked the products that are sent every month. So Barkbox's NSM can reasonably be monthly recurring revenue.

REMEMBER

Software as a Service (SaaS) businesses can also measure recurring revenue, but more often than not it's easier to track actual user actions via analytics tools that deliver value because the products are online — as opposed to ones like Barkbox, where the value delivery is offline. (See Chapter 4 for more on the use of analytics tools.)

When there may be low frequency of usage for your product

It's reasonably common to have a product that is used infrequently. Take travel sites — how often do most regular people take a vacation every year?

Just because you have a low frequency use case doesn't mean that your NSM needs to change. For example, Airbnb's NSM would be the number of nights booked. Just because neither you nor I travel more than three or four times a year for vacation and Airbnb doesn't know how many nights we might travel doesn't mean that this NSM has to change. After all, we'd only book nights on Airbnb if we found the service valuable. The company is reducing friction by providing more choice and sometimes cheaper prices than staying at a comparable hotel. If we saw either of these value propositions not being satisfied, we might look elsewhere, but if the value propositions are in fact there, then we continue to book nights and Airbnb (and the hosts) continues to make money. The only difference is that Airbnb has to work a little harder to keep its brand popping up across various acquisition channels for new and returning customers in order to raise the odds that, when people think of booking a room, they think of Airbnb first.

REMEMBER

Any low frequency product would behave similarly, whether it's a home buying product, like Zillow, or car insurance, like Geico.

When there may be no set frequency of usage or more than one way to derive value from your product

In the event that your product's usage doesn't fall neatly into any bucket of frequency usage and/or has more than one way to derive value, you still have options.

TIP

When you have a complex product, evaluate whether what Facebook does works for your product. Facebook defines users as active as long as they perform a discrete set of actions. It doesn't (seem to) particularly care whether you perform one action all the time or more than one of them, because all of them deliver value to you in some combination.

Would coming up with your own definition of *active* solve for this? Well, I'd say to some extent. Unlike Facebook, you may not have a set usage frequency, but that doesn't mean you shouldn't strive for your customers to have one. Think about it: If you didn't use a product you paid for at least once a month in some way, would you think it was providing value to you? This is where you might expand the value of *active* so that it would include users who read notifications or reports that show progress toward some value that your customers care about. They may or may not act on this information, but this allows you the opportunity to consider *active* within, at least, a monthly time frame.

Maybe your product has a special low-frequency use case that needs interaction only once a quarter or once a year. Again, that doesn't change the fact that if you provide something that indicates the value of your product for when it will be used, you raise the odds of it actually being used and delivering on that value.

A company I worked at, The Predictive Index, is a great example. Its product is a talent optimization platform that has different features for different stages of hiring and retaining talent. Various features deliver value at different times and on no set frequency, simply because hiring and talent retention activities are always ongoing. It had an added issue where different types of users could extract different value — HR managers versus line managers, for example.

The complexity of the product posed a problem when it came to determining the NSM, but the company solved this issue by coming up with its own definition of *active.* Essentially, it assigned scores to each value-generating activity, because some actions were really more valuable than others. These activities were then tied to the annual subscription amount for the product. What the company ended up with was a custom NSM that was a ratio of the subscription amount and the activity score — a Dollars/Activity score, in other words.

The thinking underlying this approach was that if customers didn't use the product enough on an ongoing basis, they wouldn't see enough value to renew their subscriptions. The smaller this Dollars/Activity score ratio, the greater the value delivered. By monitoring the trend of this value, they'd not only be able to see the overall NSM trend but also be agile about identifying which customers were at risk with higher ratios and undertake activities to provide more value, thus moving the overall NSM.

Understanding How Your Product Grows Today

Understanding the importance of an NSM and having a way to identify it is crucial, but you also need to understand the variables that may impact this number — variables that are all part of the customer journey. (For more on the customer journey, see Chapter 5.) It is important now to understand how these variables work together to impact your NSM. If you can understand the relationship between these variables, you'll be able to see where your next opportunities for growth might come from. In other words, a growth model is nothing but the customer journey with data.

For most products and businesses, growing the NSM is a function of three factors:

>> Number of customers

>> Average order/contract/transaction value

>> Retention (or lifetime value)

To impact one or more of these factors, you can run tests across the entire customer journey, if you want, but that starts getting messy quickly. You need a systematic way to attack the right part of the journey for maximal gain. A growth model helps you understand where those opportunities may lie and also gives you a way to communicate why coming up with such a model makes sense to others in the company.

WARNING

It's easy as a growth professional to start working on the top of the funnel because that's most easily understood by most executives. However, if you do that without understanding the aha moment and the core product value (I explain what this is in the next section), you're potentially wasting time, money, and effort by bringing more people into a product experience where you haven't learned about what will get people to use your product and stick around for the long term. You may also be focusing on an area that doesn't need your effort at this time, leading to massive opportunity cost along with all that wasted effort.

A Simple Growth Equation

A *growth model* helps you predict how customers find out about the product and their journey through experiencing the value of the product, buying it, and then telling others about how great it is.

Many growth models are out there, but Johns recommends one specific equation. (See Figure 6-1.)

FIGURE 6-1:
The Andy Johns
growth equation.

Top of Funnel (traffic, conversion rates)	×	Magic Moment (create emotional response)	×	Core Product Value (solves real problems)	=	Sustainable Growth

This high-level equation helps you see how your product grows over time. This list describes the three pieces:

>> **Top of the funnel:** Represents all the ways people find out about and buy your product, whether that's online or offline (search engine optimization, ads, social media, or content marketing, for example).

>> **Magic moment:** Represents a customer's first experience, or the "aha moment," where they understand the value of your product. Just as every product's NSM is different, the magic moment will similarly be different — making connections in a social product, accessing a dashboard for a productivity tool, or comparing ticket prices on an airline aggregator, for example. This also includes the key steps people take to experience the magic moment.

>> **Core product value:** Represents the problem your product is solving for its customers. It's related to a certain action they take that accomplishes this and also includes the key steps that people have to take in order to experience that core value.

To translate John's equation into something usable, you need to write down the key steps of the customer journey and for each step get data (or the best estimate) for it. For example, for an SaaS and an e-commerce example, you might see something like this:

SaaS product growth = (Top of funnel) traffic to landing pages × trial sign-up rate × trial user activities (aha moment) × trial to paid conversion rate × paid user activities (core product value)

E-commerce growth = (Top of funnel) traffic to site × account registration rate × first product purchase (aha moment) × purchases in multiple categories × repeat purchase behavior (core product value)

This is clearly more detailed than Johns's formula, but this is to be expected because the formula is just a guide for you to plug in your specific scenario. The idea here is that you can apply the formula at an even more detailed level to get a more granular understanding of your model.

To see what I'm getting at, check out how the formula works for an entity like Quora. To do that, start with the last part of the equation first. Which core value am I talking about here? For Quora, the core value for users lies in being able to find high quality answers to questions. After you have established that fact, all you need to do is document the sequence of steps you'd take to get to that point. It might look something like this:

1. You go to the Quora site (top of funnel).
2. You create an account, which includes picking topic categories of interest to you.
3. You see a feed of questions related to the topics you are interested in.
4. You click on a question and read high quality responses (aha moment).
5. You click on a second question and read more answers.
6. You are prompted to provide an answer to a question, which you do.
7. The next day you get an email from Quora with links to questions you may be interested in.
8. You click through to a question and read its answers (core value).

You can represent this in equation form this way:

Quora growth = Top of funnel traffic to Quora site × Sign up rate × Interacting with 1st question (aha moment) × Interacting with 2nd question × Answering a question × Click through rate from email back to Quora site × Watching more videos (core product value)

If you were tasked with expanding growth for Quora, you'd now have a better understanding of the key actions that drive growth — information that would allow you to make smarter decisions about your biggest growth levers.

This, however, would be just the start of your activities. The power of growth models to impact your NSM is multiplied when you can segment your data by channel and type of users. It's highly unlikely that users who come to you from

Facebook will behave the same as ones who come from a Google search. The same could be true of desktop users versus mobile users. If that is the case, what's different? Which is better? Who gets further along in the customer journey? Who buys more (or more quickly)? Who refers others the most? Look at your growth model and ask yourself whether the key inputs are the same across all user bases or are different among different groups.

REMEMBER

Getting the answers to these kinds of questions is crucial because the clearer you define your growth equation for different customer segments instead of in aggregate, the better you'll be able to unlock insights you can act on.

REMEMBER

Though a growth model can help you better understand how your product grows, no growth model will ever be perfect. Every model has some assumptions built into it because, in reality, you rarely have all the data all the time. All you can do is to get as much real data as possible. In other words, don't stress yourself out by trying to find a model that is 100 percent accurate.

If you can't wait to give the whole growth model concept a shot, Chris More, the former head of product growth and analytics at Firefox, created a growth model template to help you understand the inputs and outcomes that could impact your product's growth. It's a bit more involved than what I lay out in this chapter, but it should be easy to see what data you need in order to create your own model. You can access it at http://bit.ly/CMGrowthModel.

REMEMBER

The true power of the growth model is as a focusing mechanism. You use it to help prioritize decisions in a data-driven way versus the opinion of the most influential person at your organization. You will use also use it to set realistic estimates for team goals, because the growth team will have a better sense of the work required to achieve their objectives. Most importantly, it instills a sense of urgency into the work the team does because they can now see how every action is in the service of growing the value delivered to your customers.

Chapter **7**

Identifying Potential Opportunities for Growth

Folks like to say, "Opportunities are everywhere." That may be true, but a lot of folks also waste a lot of time looking for the wrong opportunity in the wrong places. In this chapter, you get a chance to look at the parts of the customer journey that either present the highest leverage opportunities or show you where the biggest problems lie. If you're looking for opportunities, these are areas you need to look at first. Putting it bluntly, you need to figure out how you can meet your growth goals within these specific areas. There are many ways you can do that, but you need to start somewhere. That starting point is all about developing an informed hypothesis that will help you focus on achieving those goals.

Narrowing Your Sights

Think of the act of focusing in the same way as aiming a camera. When you're trying to take a picture, the lens is moving in and out so that it can better capture the object you're interested in. Objectives are just like that: They're an outcome you're interested in that you then associate with specific experiments to see whether they can help you achieve the outcome you want.

One way to help you focus on the outcomes you want is to make use of a framework that helps you visualize the potential for growth. I'm a fan of Dave McClure's AARRR funnel — also known as *Pirate Metrics.* (For more on the AARRR funnel, see Chapter 4.)

The AARRR funnel looks like the one you see in Figure 7-1, showing Acquisition, Activation, Retention, Referral, and Revenue. These simple questions help define the terms:

>> **Acquisition:** How are your prospective customers finding out about your product?

>> **Activation:** What convinces a prospective customer of the value of your product?

>> **Retention:** How do your customers keep experiencing the value of your product?

>> **Referral:** What inspires your customers to talk about your product with others?

>> **Revenue:** What prompts your customers to pay for your product?

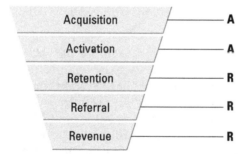

FIGURE 7-1:
Dave McClure's
Pirate Metrics.

Now assume that a rigorous analysis of your growth model has shown you that the biggest conversion-rate drop was between the Acquisition and Activation steps. In other words, you have lots of people showing up on your site, but not many of them are getting to their "aha" moment about your product — that moment when they realize your product is uniquely qualified to fill one of their needs. Suppose that the end result of that aha moment, were it to occur, would be to register on your site.

The hypothesis follows that, if you were to move more people to their aha moment, more people would sign up on your site. This becomes your area of focus. This becomes your objective. You'd start your objective creation process by writing down a statement like this one:

Objective: Increase sign-ups for the product

Great, but how would you measure success for this objective?

I find it helpful to use the Who/What/When/Where structure for fleshing out the boundaries for success:

>> **Where:** You're talking about sign-ups as a result of a great first experience and about first-time visitors so this is wherever this action happens on your site or app.

>> **What:** This element has multiple questions to help you identify where you're starting from and where you want to end up. So, you're asking these questions:

What is being measured?

What is the starting point?

What change can I expect to see as a result of running tests against this objective?

In this case, you measure daily registrations. The starting point is, say, five registrations per day. You expect to see that change impact overall registrations by 400 percent, so you expect to see registrations go, on average, from 5 to 20.

>> **When:** When will you start measuring this objective, and when will you stop? (This stage simply identifies the start and end dates for this objective.)

>> **Who:** Who on the team is responsible for managing the progress against this objective?

Now, if you wrote this objective systematically, you could use this format:

Objective: Increase new visitor sign-ups

Start date: MM/DD/YY

End date: MM/DD/YY

Metric: Daily registrations

Current measurement: Five registrations/day

Expected change (%): 400%

Daily or weekly change (#): 20 registrations/day

Owner: Anuj Adhiya

"THE MARTIAN"

If you've seen the 2015 movie *The Martian,* you'll remember that it's the story of an astronaut, played by Matt Damon, who ends up being stranded on Mars. The entire story is about his figuring out how to return to Earth. His goal, and his measurable North Star Metric, was, "Be rescued by my team," because he didn't have a rocket to use to return home. This goal was his What. To enable that, he needed to figure out, of course, how to stay alive long enough to achieve his goal. So staying alive until he was rescued naturally became his objective. This is what he absolutely had to focus on in order to achieve his goal. Given that his character was also a scientist, he rapidly employed the scientific method and started experimenting with different ways to figure out how to stay alive long enough to be rescued.

If you haven't seen the movie yet, I won't spoil the ending for you, but most of the movie is about his running experiments focused around a singular, important objective that would impact his North Star Metric. So, whether you're talking about *The Martian* or growth, the fundamental truth of the need for focus and a systematic method of learning is exactly the same.

Now you and everyone else on the team are clear on the focus of tests for the next period and why. By definition, tests you decide to prioritize in this period should all help you achieve the agreed-on objective. If other ideas do not map to this objective, by all means add them to your backlog, though they cannot be considered at this time.

REMEMBER

Everything about growth hacking is meant to be iterative — you have to keep doing what you do, time and again. This applies similarly to the time frame you pick for achieving your objectives. You have to provide enough time for you to see the impact on your testing, but you also want to stay on top of the changes you're effecting as well.

A good starting point for determining how much time you should spend focusing on an objective is at least 30 days. Within this period, you should start to see whether you're having an impact on your objective metric. You may not get all the way there, but if you're moving in the right direction, you should extend that by another 30 days. Within 60 days, you definitely should be getting close to consistently meeting or beating your objective metric. If you look at your data and are still growing the impact on your objective metric, extend it for another 30 days. At the 90-day mark, you may find that you have extracted most of the value from the tests. You will know this because you won't see meaningful gains week after week in your objective metric, like you did in earlier weeks. You have to decide whether it's worth your effort to continue to focus on this objective or whether it would be better to return to the growth model and find the next biggest area to attack.

If at any time during these 30-day chunks you find that you aren't impacting your objective metrics — or are impacting them negatively — stop running these tests immediately. This is your signal to come up with a new objective within the same part of the AARRR funnel that has the biggest opportunity or problem and then run different tests.

TIP

If you find that you have multiple areas of opportunity or problems that need to be addressed simultaneously (which is normal), set objectives for each of these areas and remember that the purpose of an objective is to provide a focus. Given that fact, you shouldn't have more than two or three objectives at the same time. If you do, by definition, you've lost your focus and need to reprioritize your objectives for impact.

TIP

A great way to jump-start the idea process is to gather the entire team (or, if it's manageable, the entire company) for an hour-long brainstorming session. The CEO *must* be part of this meeting. Within this session, to provide context, spend ten minutes sharing the North Star Metric, growth model analysis, and the objective(s) based on that analysis. Then ask everyone to write down at least five ideas on sticky notes that they believe can impact the objective metrics. At the end of the session, you should have a good backlog of ideas on which you can start to develop hypotheses and prioritize to begin testing.

Choosing the Best Ideas to Test

After you've settled on an objective, all the ideas you test should map back to impacting that objective metric. This brings up the question of how you're supposed to come up with ideas to test. (If you've never done this, it can seem to be a rather daunting task.)

REMEMBER

Growth is a collaborative process — don't restrict idea generation to yourself or just a few people. The more people who participate, the more ideas and perspectives you'll have to test. Actively solicit input from people to help build your backlog.

In my experience, you can go about coming up with ideas to test in two main ways:

>> Internal data

>> External inspiration, from competition and sources unrelated to your business

The following sections take a look at both methods.

Internal data

A macro-level analysis of your customer journey can reveal your areas of biggest opportunity or your biggest problems (as described in Chapter 6). That same process can be used to look at the customer journey at the micro-level. Again, though you have a number of different ways to look at the customer journey, I focus here on user flow insights and user experience insights.

User flow insights

Looking at user flow involves mapping out granularly every step that someone has to take to accomplish a goal. What you're doing here is looking deeply within the step of the AARRR funnel against which you have set your objective. You're trying to see what it is, exactly, that you're making people do. What buttons do they have to click? What fields do they have to fill out (see Figure 7-2)?

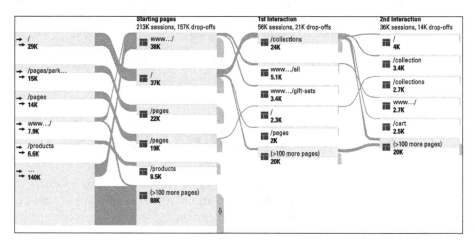

FIGURE 7-2: Sample user flow with metrics.

If the step you're solving for is Acquisition, you're also looking at what channels you're using and what you're doing in each channel in the hope of driving traffic to your product or landing pages. This helps you segment data to find out the efficiency of each channel as it relates to any conversion events downstream, like signing up, requesting a demo, or becoming a repeat user.

At the end of this process, you should have a flow diagram that lays out every step someone undertakes that you can then map data to. Your analytics tools are your most important source to get this data, but you may discover — especially when you do this the first time — that you don't have all the data for the steps you've laid out. This becomes your trigger to go and gather this data, to give you more clarity on what specific steps are opportunities or problems you can test ideas against.

User experience insights

A good way to get an additional data point on which step(s) to experiment against is to complete the same steps you want other people to take. I can almost guarantee that you will be surprised at what you make people do in order to buy or use your product.

This process helps you look at the customer journey through a new person's eyes and gauge the level of difficulty with each step. As you approach the part of the journey that's associated with your objective, you'll have insight into what they've experienced beforehand. This is important context when thinking about where they might be stumbling in the area you're interested in. If your product has a mobile app, repeat this process for both web and app experiences. If a user has multiple ways to sign up, walk through each step of doing this in order to identify opportunities. Leave no stone unturned.

TIP

If you're focusing on Acquisition, you also want to evaluate all your current channels and determine the sequence of steps you expect people to follow to find out about you before using your product. Complete those exact steps of searching and learning and see whether they make sense and whether you find any gaps in how someone goes from knowing nothing about you to ending up with your product.

Going through this process should help confirm what the user flow insights show you as areas you should test in. They may also reveal other gaps, anomalies, or flaws that aren't obvious in the data and help you come up with more ideas to test.

External inspiration

Just as you look at your data to get ideas for tests, other companies have undertaken the same process. This is especially true of more mature companies, which have likely run hundreds of tests to optimize their customer journeys. Use their hard work to your advantage.

You can do this analysis not only with your competitors but also with products you like and use regularly. The best part about growth is that you never know what will work until you test it. So, just because a product doesn't compete with you doesn't mean that you can't gather ideas for tests from them. This happened all the time when I was at GrowthHackers, and, despite our high tempo of testing, we ended up with a backlog of over a thousand untested ideas at any given point. Figure 7-3 shows an example of a new user to-do list idea, copied from Quora and tested out to great success.

FIGURE 7-3:
GrowthHackers
To-Do List
example, copied
from Quora.

Just as you undertook the customer journey with your own product, do the same with other products. Look at the marketing copy and calls to action (CTAs) on their landing pages. Create test accounts for their websites so that you can see what a new user experience is like. Find out how they try to build a habit for their product. What do their emails or mobile push notifications look like? As Bill Watterson, the creator of *Calvin and Hobbes,* said, "There's treasure everywhere!"

REMEMBER

As part of this process, don't ignore what the fastest-growing companies are doing and have done. Companies like Facebook, Airbnb, and Pinterest have all run thousands of tests in an attempt to optimize their customer journeys. Plenty of smart people have been involved in testing at these places, which makes them another great source of testable ideas.

Ensuring That You Have a Good Hypothesis

If you're like most people, reading this heading is probably among the few times you've heard or read the word *hypothesis* outside of a science context. It's not surprising in the context of growth hacking, though, because the methodology largely follows the scientific method.

WARNING

You *must* explicitly state a hypothesis before testing. When you run tests, you need surety about their outcome. Did the test work? Agreeing on a hypothesis upfront makes it a lot easier to say whether the test was a success. It's all well and good for you to have an idea in your head about what you're trying to prove, but if you don't state it explicitly, different people will have different ideas for what success or failure of a test means. This, in turn, leads to lots of wasted time, which then leads to frustration with testing in general. This kills momentum.

The potential for learning the right results from your test greatly depends on the strength of your hypotheses. It follows that a good hypothesis should give you insights, whatever the outcome. The possible outcomes are that the hypothesis will be a) proven, b) disproven, or c) inconclusive. Based on the outcome, you will have more information on ideas for future tests.

With that in mind, let's take a look at what makes a good hypothesis. In my view, a good hypothesis has three essential characteristics:

>> It is something you can test.

>> It measures a change or difference.

>> Its results provide insights for the next steps.

If you had to translate this into a simple hypothesis statement, here's a simple way to lay it out:

Because we saw *[data/feedback]*,

we expect that *[change]* will cause *[impact]*.

We'll measure this using *[metric]*.

In fact, this was the format I used during my time at GrowthHackers, and it worked very well.

Examples of a good (and a bad) hypothesis

Say that you thought your home page needed a new *call to action* — the affirmative step you want the visitor or user to take.

Your reasoning goes like this: A new call to action might well increase sign-ups. Worded as a hypothesis, you might say, "Changing the call to action on the home page will increase sign-ups."

Now put this hypothesis within the structure I laid out at the end of the preceding section:

Because we saw *[data/feedback]*,

we expect that *changing the call to action on the home page* will cause more sign-ups.

We'll measure this using *[metric]*.

You'll notice that all we were able to fill out was just one aspect of the hypothesis. Some gaps still need filling because the hypothesis isn't specific enough yet. It doesn't yet satisfy the characteristics of being testable and measuring a change. In other words, this is not a good hypothesis.

To turn around this not-at-all good hypothesis, you need to answer these questions:

» What have I seen that tells me that this is a test I should perform?

» Where on the home page should I add this call to action?

» What does the current call to action say?

» What should the new call to action say?

» Why should it say something different?

» What is the change I am expecting, and how will it be measured?

If you answer these questions and return to the hypothesis template, you'd be able to come up with something like this:

Because we saw *confusion regarding how to register a demo from our live chat transcripts,*

we expect that *changing the call to action copy from Sign Up to Request Demo* will cause more demo registrations.

We'll measure this using *# of demo sign-ups.*

Your newly formulated hypothesis answers all the questions and makes clear what you're going to do and why, what change you'll be testing, and how you'll measure it. The results will also point to other tests you will run. You now have a good hypothesis.

Surveys and research are precursors to tests

When I first started running tests, I was under the impression that any activity I completed that gave me more ideas for future tests was also a test in itself. This was based on my misunderstanding of what a testable hypothesis is. I neglected the parts about running a test and measuring a change and focused just on the bit about its outcomes providing insights for future tests. I got caught up in the fallacy that just because I was doing something that gave me more insights for tests, I was actually running tests. In reality, I was doing research, which was important pre-work, just not a test.

This research is important because it gives you qualitative data. Quantitative data, which you get from your analytics tools, is useful for telling you what is happening. It cannot answer why, however. Qualitative data provides this key. Knowing *why* people do what they do means that you know more about their motivations and goals. This is a foundational element of growth hacking because, if you understand what people are trying to achieve, it becomes easier to come up with ways to serve up what they really want, rather than what *you* think is a great product experience.

This list describes a couple of easy ways to get started with research:

>> **Customer interviews:** The best way to gather insights from people is to interview them. You can do this online, on the phone, or in person. As you conduct more interviews, you'll soon discover that one approach works better for your than others, so do what works for you.

Narrow your focus so that you interview only ten individuals who match your ideal customer profile. In other words, these are the customers who get the most value from your product and for whom your product is most suited for. If you could find more of them, you'll surely have boosted your growth.

Simple tools like Google Forms or Typeform will suffice here.

>> **Online surveys:** These are surveys you can run on your site or app to give you more insight into the user experience. Tools like Qualaroo or Hotjar are good choices here. (See Figure 7-4 for a sample question.)

Such surveys almost always have open-ended questions. Sometimes, they might have multiple-choice questions if you know that you want specific responses. Because these are on your site or app, you can (and should) gather more responses, to give you more information on patterns of behavior — ideally, somewhere in the region of 100 to 250 responses. That should give you enough information about the general direction of the responses.

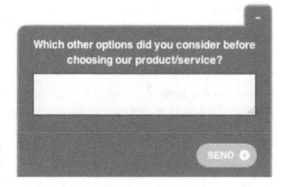

FIGURE 7-4:
A sample online survey.

Whether you're dealing with person-to-person interviews or online surveys, you have to come up with the right questions, and by that I mean questions that yield useful answers. Otherwise, you'll find yourself in a garbage-in, garbage-out situation.

In general, you're trying to find the answers to these questions:

>> **Who are these people?**

This helps you understand personas.

>> **What is their goal?**

This helps you understand their motivations and what kinds of problems they're looking to solve for themselves.

>> **What matters to them?**

This helps you understand what exactly they are looking for in a product that they believe will help them achieve their goal.

>> **What's stopping them from taking the next step?**

This is everything that makes them think twice about the next step and prevents them from trying or buying your product — fears, doubts, and hesitations they experienced before making the purchase.

Putting this into practice will give you questions like these:

>> How do you briefly describe yourself (or your business)?

>> What problem does *[your product]* solve for you?

>> What improvements have you seen as a result?

>> What alternatives did you consider?

>> What finally convinced you to sign up for our product?

>> What, if anything, almost prevented you from signing up for our product?

>> What questions are still left unanswered for you?

>> Is there anything else you want to tell us?

I've found that it's best to ask seven or eight questions per survey. It's not too many to kill the response rate, yet not too few to render the process useless.

TIP

When running surveys online, you cannot ask more than one question at a time, because no one will sit still for that. Pick a single question that will be most impactful to your learning, and stick with it. On the other hand, when conducting customer interviews, you can ask all these questions together, because you will have set aside 15 to 30 minutes, for this purpose, anyway.

The great part about such surveys is that they reveal patterns in words that people use. These are words you can then use in your product and marketing copy to attract other people who resonate with this same language.

REMEMBER

Make no mistake: Reviewing survey responses is time consuming, but it's critical that you do it. Without this exercise, you will never get a granular understanding of how to impact the growth of your business.

Seeing How the Pieces Fit Together

In Chapter 9, I talk more about the specifics of tests, but before you drill down into that topic, it's important to clarify how the concepts of the North Star Metric, your own objectives, and tests are related.

Keep in mind the specific hierarchy here to help you stay focused on the most impactful actions for growth. Recall that the North Star Metric is the number that quantifies the value you deliver to your customers. Everything you do is in the service of growing this value. *Objectives* are areas of focus within your customer journey that you believe can positively impact your North Star Metric. *Tests* are activities you use to help you achieve your objectives.

To put it simply: North Star Metric ⇨ Objectives ⇨ Tests.

It follows, then, that if you choose the right tests, you raise the odds of producing a meaningful result that helps grow your business. When your tests are oriented toward improving your North Star Metric, you'll be able to focus the entire team on building better hypotheses and creating strong experiments you can learn from.

When I first started running tests at GrowthHackers, I ran them based on the potential that those tests had to move the company's North Star Metric. I found that I achieved many small wins and gained lots of insights, but I wasn't impacting the North Star Metric in any meaningful way.

It turned out that two factors were at play:

>> I hadn't done a good enough job of analyzing the company's growth model in order to come up with the right objectives to use when focusing tests.

>> I hadn't set a time frame that I could use effectively to measure the overall impact of the tests I was running. In hindsight, I could see that I ran tests haphazardly across the entire customer journey, which ended up giving me small lifts in conversions all over the place, but these particular tests didn't have a chance to compound and consolidate their impact in a way that would grow the North Star Metric meaningfully.

When the company introduced objectives into the process, the situation changed. Other than the focus benefits that I outline earlier in this chapter, I was amazed at the power of objectives in making our testing more agile. When later tests were run, one of three things took place:

>> Tests did not impact the objective metric positively — they stayed the same or grew worse — which meant that the North Star Metric wasn't impacted positively.

>> Tests impacted the objective metric positively, but the North Star Metric wasn't impacted positively.

>> Tests impacted the objective metric positively, and the North Star Metric was impacted positively.

Here's the where the brilliance of objectives began to shine. I can tell you now that if you encounter the first scenario, you don't need to wait the full 30 days to understand what's going on. You will likely start to see, within a couple of weeks of testing, that nothing positive is happening to the objective or your North Star Metric. If this happens, you need to make a call on whether it's worth your effort to continue testing or better to stop immediately, return to your growth model, and find a different objective.

The second scenario shows exactly the same thing. It's all well and good to be crushing your objective metric, but if that isn't having an impact on your North Star Metric, it's also a sign that you're focused on the wrong area (at this time). Again, go back to your growth model and find a different objective to test.

In both of these scenarios, without the lens of objectives, you would likely continue testing and testing until you saw some movement in your North Star Metric. Your decisions on future tests would also come much later, making you slower to respond to your growth opportunities.

The last scenario is what you're looking for. You know you're focused on the right objective when you're moving your objective metric and North Star Metric positively as you continue to test. You should still evaluate, as you hit 30 days, whether it's worth the effort to continue testing around the current objective. Now, however, you have more certainty that the testing you're doing is having the right impact at the right place within your customer journey, because you can measure that impact within your objective metric as well as your North Star Metric.

Chapter **8**

Prioritizing Your Ideas before You Test Them

Understanding the general framework of growth hacking — the importance of your product's North Star Metric, the customer journey, and your own objectives — is a crucial first step in any growth program, but the real work begins when you start testing. The objectives you pick give you a potentially high-impact area to test within. However, they don't tell you which tests within that focus area to run first. Therefore, you need a way to prioritize tests that everyone on the growth team can understand and agree on. Of course, launching tests is just the start. Once you've run them, you want to ensure the appropriate analysis to glean the right insights that light the way to your next round of tests. This process of prioritizing, launching, analyzing tests, and coming up with new ideas — paired with adjusting for new objectives when needed — will form the core of your growth program moving forward.

The Importance of Prioritization

It goes without saying that a precursor to prioritizing ideas is to have a backlog to select from. (See Chapter 7 for more on creating such a backlog.) I'd recommend a backlog of at least 20 ideas before you start your testing program. You should also understand *why* you need to prioritize testing before getting into *how* you do it.

It's easy to understand that prioritization provides focus. You really don't want to be doing aimless testing. You want to always have clarity on which idea you're testing, why you're testing it, and why this idea was picked versus another one to run first.

A good prioritization framework also offers a few more benefits. The biggest one is that it brings transparency to the growth process. When you pick tests based on predefined criteria, it's easy for everyone to get on board with a test that's being performed. This helps you avoid falling into the HiPPO (Highest Paid Person's Opinion) trap.

TECHNICAL STUFF

Avinash Kaushik coined the acronym HiPPO in his book *Web Analytics: An Hour a Day*. HiPPOs tend to be those who have the most experience or the greatest power (or both) in the growth meeting. And, once this opinion is voiced, depending on the organizational culture, it can be difficult to speak up against it. When a HiPPO is in effect, you're not relying on data and evidence to make decisions, but rather on what the HiPPO wants and feels should get done. The impact of the HiPPO cannot be understated in its ability to drag you off course and negatively impact your entire growth program.

You tackle the HiPPO with data. Data depersonalizes decision-making by removing the emotion associated with it. Now it's not about anyone thinks — it's about the facts. You should be able find data to support your position internally from information already available to you or, if that isn't an option, from external examples that can help guide decisions.

TIP

If you're the HiPPO in the meeting, the first step is self-awareness of the impact you can have on the growth process. So, it's up to you to ensure that a culture where opinions are sought and encouraged flourishes. Invite contrary opinions. Designate a devil's advocate in the room, if you have to. This strategy helps everyone realize that they don't need to be afraid of the HiPPO and that they can have as much influence on growth as any HiPPO out there.

As a result of mitigating the HiPPO, you can set the right expectations around the growth process. By that, I mean that all tests can be evaluated based on a hypothesis and the same prioritization criteria. This way, everyone knows the "rules of engagement" — a state of affairs that not only helps the team operate in a standardized way but also gives management more confidence in the plan you've chosen to execute.

Lastly, but no less important a consideration, is one of opportunity cost. Every test you run is costing you in terms of time, money, and learning. Your prioritization method should raise the odds of picking tests that have the highest potential, in terms of either generating a win or learning something significant. This gains even more importance as you realize that picking a test that could yield little of real value to run also means costs associated with prepping this experiment, following through to its conclusion, and ultimately determining, when all is said and done, that you picked the wrong test to run with.

Now that you understand why you need to prioritize tests, let's dive into how you can prioritize them with the help of objective frameworks.

Methodologies for Prioritizing Ideas

You've brainstormed some new ideas, and you've built up a good backlog. Now it's time to put some thought into which ones to test first. I present some common frameworks for making that decision here, but you're probably already aware that there's no such thing as a truly perfect system. I also list them in order of increasing complexity. You and your team should evaluate what works best for you — don't be afraid about switching the way you prioritize ideas if one way isn't doing the job.

The ICE score

Sean Ellis popularized the ICE score and we used this at GrowthHackers.com. It's also the one I use when introducing teams to the growth methodology, because it's a simple concept to grasp.

ICE stands for:

>> **Impact:** What is the potential impact of this test?

>> **Confidence:** How confident am I that this will work?

>> **Ease:** What is the ease of implementation?

Each of these variables can be scored from 1 to 10, with 1 the lowest score and 10 the highest. Averaging the individual scores gives you the overall ICE score. Ideas with the highest ICE score get a chance to be tested first. (See Figure 8-1.)

FIGURE 8-1:
An ICE score
example.

> **6.7**
> Impact 4
> Confidence 7
> Ease 9

Impact scores are a function of your analytics, where traffic, important interactions, pages that contribute a lot of value to your customers, potential to convert, and insights from customer feedback inform how high the score might be. You're using as much data as you have, and the more you find yourself guessing, the lower the score.

TIP

A quick way to determine an impact score is to start at 5 if it's a high-traffic or high-importance page, and to start at 1 if it's not. Add one point from there on out for as many supporting data points you may have.

Your Confidence score stems from the same kind of information you use to estimate Impact. To make this easy, start out at 5 as well and add one point for every discrete piece of data you have that supports your hypothesis. Confidence can be lower if this is the first time you're testing a radical change to your product, but if this is a follow-on test meant to double-down on a signal from an earlier test, this score is another data point that you can add to your score.

TIP

If you have no internal data and are using external inspiration — say, something you saw recently with another product — leave the score at 5. The odds are really at 50 percent here because every product exists within its own context. If you're just guessing, start at 4 if you think it's a good guess based on experience with another product. If it's a pure guess, start at 3 and go lower based on whether you yourself have low conviction.

The Ease score is a measure of effort to launch the test. The more time and people involved, the lower the Ease score. If it's something you can do quickly on your own, give it a 9 or 10. If it's something that needs approval but doesn't need anybody else to do any actual work, it's likely around 7 or 8. Beyond that, the score decreases as more people get involved who need to do work like design or coding.

REMEMBER

I'll be the first to admit that the ICE score isn't the perfect system for prioritizing individual ideas. It's intended to be a system of relative prioritization (which all prioritization frameworks should be). What that means is that you're not using it to decide whether you should run a test as much as which test to run first. The goal is to prevent you from being bogged down in trying to fine-tune the score too much. Think of the ICE score as a minimum viable prioritization framework. It's not objectively perfect, but it's good enough to get the job done.

The PIE framework

Chris Goward of WiderFunnel came up with this framework. It's like the ICE score in that that it includes three variables that you assign scores from 1 to 10. (See Figure 8-2.) Those variables are

>> **Potential:** How much improvement can be made on the pages?

>> **Importance:** How valuable is the traffic to the pages?

>> **Ease:** How hard will it be to launch the test (resources, technical difficulty, and number of stakeholders, for example)?

Again, the ideas with the higher PIE scores would be first in line to be tested.

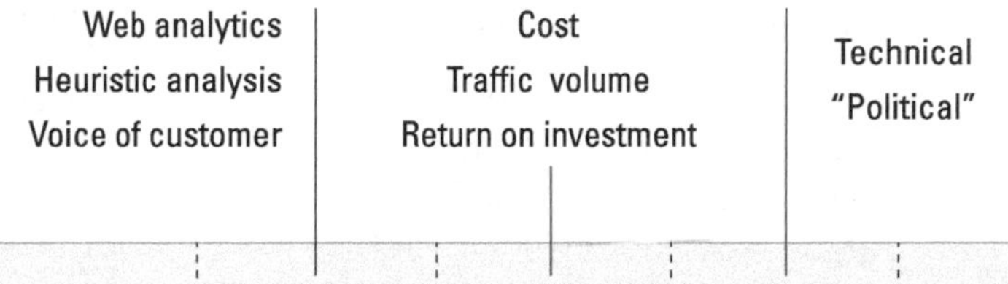

	Web analytics Heuristic analysis Voice of customer	Cost Traffic volume Return on investment	Technical "Political"	
LIFT zone	Potential	Importance	Ease	PIE score
Homepage	10	10	8	9.3
Checkout	8	10	9	9.0
Product page	10	9	7	8.7

FIGURE 8-2: A PIE framework example.

A Potential score — asking how much you can improve a given page, screen, or flow — is useful because it gets you thinking that you need to compare data among alternatives and make a call.

An Importance score — asking how valuable the traffic to a page or screen is as a function of the volume of traffic, cost of that traffic, and impact on conversions — helps you put your efforts in perspective. Looking at traffic through multiple lenses — including lenses that include the directness of their role in delivering value — helps you develop a better sense of how to score this factor versus looking at it just from a volume-and-cost basis.

The Ease score, by asking how much time and effort it will take to launch the test, helps the team understand the scope of work required to launch a test and set the right expectations for when it will launch.

There are no hard-and-fast rules when it comes to how you assign scores here. The goal remains to quickly identify higher-priority tests and make it easy for others to participate. So, in general, everything I've just mentioned about the benefits of the ICE score applies here as well.

The TIR score

Bryan Eisenberg, a pioneer of online marketing, came up with the TIR score — Time, Impact, and Resources — as a general way to prioritize any type of project, ranking each variable from 1 to 5:

>> **Time:** How many calendar days or person hours do you estimate it would take to a) launch a test and b) have it be able to achieve its maximum impact? You assign a score of 5 to any test that would take the least amount of time to launch and to realize its impact.

>> **Impact:** How much will revenue change (or costs decrease) if this test is successful? Here, you'd consider factors like the size of the testing population (including everyone versus including only a specific segment, for example), potential increase in conversion rates, and so on. You assign a score of 5 for tests that have the greatest positive impact on revenue or cost reduction potential.

>> **Resources:** What are the costs (people, tools, and so on) associated with launching this test? You assign a score of 5 if you need the fewest resources to launch this test. It should go without saying that resources must be available to you to be part of this consideration.

To determine your final score, you multiply the individual scores and work on the ones with the highest score first because those are estimated to have the most impact on revenue in the least amount of time and with the smallest amount of resources.

The RICE score

The RICE score (Reach, Impact, Confidence, Effort) was developed by the messaging software platform maker Intercom to aid with project management, but it applies just as well to prioritizing growth experiments. Conceptually speaking, this is just like the ICE score with the added variable for Reach and some differences in how the other variables and the final score are calculated:

- » **Reach** is the estimate of how many people or actions (like purchases) that the idea, if tested, could affect within a given period. Again, you're using the best possible data available to you to make this estimate. That means, as much as possible, use real measurements from product metrics rather than pull numbers from a hat.

- » **Impact** in this framework has a smaller scale because it can be difficult to measure precisely. If Reach were about how many people you can affect, this number is looking at the potential impact on a per-person basis, where Massive = 3, High = 2, Medium = 1, Low = 0.5, and Minimal = 0.25.

- » **Confidence** is used as a percentage where High = 100 percent, Medium = 80 percent, and Low = 50 percent. Again, the question to ask yourself here is how much data do you have for your estimate?

- » **Effort** is estimated as a function of time or person hours. The estimates are kept at whole or half numbers (3 or 3.5, for example). Obviously, the more effort it takes to launch a test, the higher the cost, so the number you've generated so far is divided by this number.

Because each variable has a different estimate measure, unlike with the ICE or PIE scores, you arrive at the final RICE number a bit differently.

The formula for the RICE score is (Reach × Impact × Confidence) ÷ Effort.

The result is a measure of Total Impact Per Hour of Work. The higher the RICE score for an idea, the bigger its priority to be tested.

REMEMBER

RICE needs a bit more work upfront, but can be helpful in cases where it's hard to decide between ideas that might have similar scores. You'll have more information on why a test might have a certain impact and whether the effort is worth it.

Hotwire's points model

Hotwire's prioritization framework was popularized by Pauline Marol and Josephine Foucher, from the Hotwire optimization team. Their framework is based on a binary scoring system that is additive: If the idea meets a requirement, it merits 1 point. If it doesn't, it merits a 0. The points are summed to give each idea an overall score out of 10. Ideas are ranked according to the overall score. The elements of this framework and how to score them are shown in Table 8-1.

TABLE 8-1　　**The Hotwire Points Model**

Rule	1 Point	0 Points
Main metric	Supports the company's main metric	Supports a secondary metric, like CTR or Net Promoter Score
Location	Tests a change to the results page or billing page	Tests a change located on any other page
Fold	Makes a change above the fold	Makes a change below the fold
Targeting	Targets 100 percent of customers	Targets a subset of customers (repeat only, new only, top 50 markets, and so on)
New information	Adds new information or a new element or removes an element from the page	Makes a change to the existing elements (copy, color, UI, and so on)
Benchmarking	Borrows from an earlier success	No benchmarking best practice
Conversion Flows	Applies to two or more conversion flows	Applies to one or fewer conversion flows
Strategic topic	Supports a strategic company goal	Doesn't map to a company-level goal
Mobile	Would change an element of the mobile web experience or encourage an app install	No mobile component
Opaque (a travel industry-specific metric related to selling unsold inventory at a discounted price)	Potential to increase opaque share for a line of business	No influence on opaque share of business

Clearly, this is a more expansive framework that needs more research to understand additional variables before you can arrive at a final score.

PXL framework

The ConversionXL team developed the PXL framework from its experience in serving multiple clients.

Like the Hotwire Points model, the PXL framework also relies on multiple data points to build a final score. It intentionally forces data gathering to be part of this process in order to make ratings more objective. If you meet specific criteria, you score a set number of points. If you don't meet any criterion, you score 0 points for it. The system also weights certain variables more heavily due to their impact. Table 8-2 summarizes the prioritization criteria and points system.

TABLE 8-2 The PXL Framework

Criteria	Points
Above the fold?	1
Noticeable within 5 seconds?	2
Adding or removing an element?	2
Designed to increase user motivation?	1
Running on high-traffic pages?	1
Addressing an issue discovered during user testing?	1
Addressing an issue discovered via qualitative feedback (polls, surveys, interviews)?	1
Addressing insights found via digital analytics?	1
Supported by mouse tracking, heat maps, or eye tracking?	1
Ease of implementation	Less than 4 hrs = 3
	Up to 8 hrs = 2
	Under 2 days =1
	More than 2 days = 0

REMEMBER

You should always use whatever system works best for you. When first starting out, you may find it easier to adopt a simpler prioritization framework and migrate to a more granular system. The potential trap in starting with a more involved system right off the bat is that you may not have ways to gather all the data needed to use those frameworks the way they were intended to be, in which case you're back to square one.

None of these methods of prioritization is 100 percent perfect, and neither do they apply to every scenario. Just as with every other part of the growth process, you should look for opportunities to optimize these frameworks to meet your needs. Your prioritization framework will and should grow as your testing program grows. In time you'll learn what kinds of tests tend to move the needle more (design changes versus copy changes, for example). Or you may find that a certain acquisition channel or customer segment is critical to the business and you add ranking criteria — whether they're binary or on a scale — to ensure that you always take those into account.

No matter which framework you use, you will encounter scenarios where the highest-scored idea isn't the one you'll consider running first. For example, your design or engineering person may be on vacation. In that case, any idea that needs such a resource is likely not getting launched in the current testing cycle. Or you may have an idea that's dependent on another idea being tested first or that it may take longer to implement a certain test with the same Impact score (however that is determined), in which case you go with the easier.

General Criticisms of Simpler Frameworks

The simpler frameworks I present in this chapter are sometimes criticized for supposedly being too subjective. Here are the general arguments:

> >> If multiple people score an idea to test, they would all score it differently.

> >> The same idea might be scored differently by the same person at different times. This difference would then affect the final prioritization list.

> >> Team members who want their tests prioritized could simply manipulate scores to get tests approved. (Let's face it, though: If you're worried about this, you have bigger problems than the wrong tests being run.)

The main criticisms are aimed at the Impact portion of these frameworks. Beyond the argument that they're too subjective, the question raised is that if you already knew the impact of the test, why would you even test it in the first place?

I have nothing against less subjective approaches, but I think the issue with these general criticisms is that they

> >> Misunderstand the purpose of the simpler frameworks

> >> Minimize or neglect the role of the growth process and the growth team

This isn't to say that the criticisms don't bring up valid points, but just because a framework isn't perfect doesn't mean it's not data-informed. Data analysis and information from past tests should inform Impact and Confidence scores. The Ease score should be a function of conversations with appropriate members of your team if you don't have specific expertise. (For more on how to carry out those conversations with your growth team, see Chapter 10.) The worst-case scenario is that you assign a score a few points higher or lower than if you had better data. But if this is a possibility, why is this nonperfect scoring of ideas not a big deal?

As you participate in the growth process, you'll find your sense of scoring becoming more fine-tuned. I use the ICE score to illustrate the point that after each test you will have real information on the impact of that test. Comparing this with the pre-test Impact score helps you understand why those differences existed. Similarly, test results will inform you whether the pre-test data you relied on for the Confidence score was adequate. Lastly, with each growth meeting, feedback on Ease scores (or developing specific expertise) tells you more about how to assign this score moving forward.

The point here is that the "good enough" characteristic of simpler ways of prioritizing tests works well because it's paired with the discipline of a growth process — as any prioritization method should be.

REMEMBER

Your ultimate decision on which ideas to test is never based on just the prioritization framework you've chosen. The purpose here is for team members to have some discipline, when they submit an idea, to think about it across a few different criteria. The more complicated you make it, the harder you make it for team members from across the company to participate in the growth process and seek areas for improvement. So, when picking a prioritization framework, think about what gives just enough friction so that, company-wide, people aren't throwing half-baked ideas for consideration, but not so much friction that they stop coming up with ideas altogether.

Chapter **9**

Testing Ideas and Learning from Them

Testing isn't a luxury or an optional activity. Because it's the only systematic and scientific way to understand where the opportunities for sustainable growth lie, testing is at the core of growth hacking.

If you have already picked out a framework for prioritizing your ideas for achieving growth (see Chapter 8 for more on that topic), you can start running tests. As a part of prioritizing ideas, you've identified potential resources, people, and time needed to test them. Now comes the fun part for everyone: learning more about what works and what doesn't and optimizing for test results that point toward the building blocks of sustainable growth.

Working with Two Types of Tests

If I have to boil down the entire growth hacking philosophy to a single sentence, it's this: Find out what works, and do more of it.

This statement tells you that you have two types of tests: one where you find out what works, and another where you do more of what's working to make it even better.

The best analogy I've come across (and tested!) that communicates this idea is one that Brian Balfour and Andrew Chen came up with, where they compared growth hacking to playing the board game *Battleship,* shown in Figure 9-1.

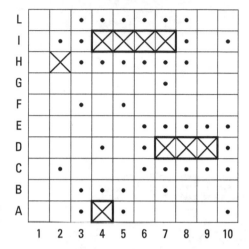

FIGURE 9-1: *Battleship* analogy.

When you start the game, you have no idea where your opponent's ships are, so you throw random missiles in noticeably different directions. Say you make your first hit on I6. You now have a signal that opportunity lies in the vicinity. Your next missile is probably I4 or I5. If neither of those hits, maybe you'll try H6 or L6. When you make your second hit, your sense of where the opportunity lies becomes even more fine-tuned, and you'd keep throwing missiles in the area to maximize your chances of a win — destroying your opponent's ship, in other words.

I like this analogy because it encapsulates some fundamental truths about growth hacking. First, you'll likely take some initial wild swings to find what works and then, after you hit pay dirt, double-down on that signal to maximize that opportunity. Those big swings allow you to more quickly learn how to win.

What you don't do is equally worth stating. When you hit your first signal at I6, you don't ignore it and throw another missile in a wildly different direction. That would make no sense. Instead, you use the data you have to inform your next steps, drawing you closer to a win.

This strategy also communicates that every opportunity is finite. After you destroy your opponent's ship, you need to find the next one. To do that, you have to start the process of finding a signal to double-down on again. Based on what you know, you may or may not start your search in the vicinity of your first success, but it's likely that you'll have to take big swings in uncharted waters again.

Lastly, it shows that winning at growth is about compounding wins over time and at a faster rate than your competition. Hitting just one ship, even if it's the biggest one, doesn't win you the game. Growth is just like that.

Prepping tests

When prioritizing ideas, set an Ease score. (See Chapter 8 for more on Ease scores.) This score informs the resources you'll need in order to launch a test. Such resources generally fall into four types of resource categories: creative, copy, engineering, and analytics. You need some combination of these resources in place before you launch that test. I summarize some key considerations here when it comes to resources, but you should know that the extent of these will vary, based on your individual circumstance.

>> **Creative:** This one applies to imagery for everything associated with the campaign — hero images (those big images at the top of pages), banners, button design, font selection, overall layout, and more. As is the case with most everything in life, you don't want to go overboard here, but you absolutely should consider what is on-brand and what is not. Sometimes, even your minimal A/B test needs to look "minimally nice."

>> **Copy:** Whether this has to do with headlines, on-page copy, call-to-action text, or some other words, you must be specific about what you're tweaking as part of your test, because it can impact everything from layout to the perception of your brand voice.

>> **Engineering:** Some tests, especially those measuring user actions that have never been tracked, need engineers to code (and/or insert) snippets at specific places as a prerequisite.

>> **Analytics:** No matter how small the test, it goes without saying that if you don't pick the right measurement tool and set up your measurement properly, you've wasted the test. You must ensure the quality of your measurement setup to ensure that goals and events are set up and "firing" correctly.

REMEMBER

When you think you've addressed all the individual pieces, rigorously inspect the entire flow of the test. If you're testing paid traffic, ensure that you've connected your ad tools to analytics and ensure that you can see users all the way to the end points you've set up. If this is an e-commerce test, verify that you can see all the transactions you're going to measure. For page elements, ensure that the test images render correctly across browsers and devices. Check that form submissions work correctly. Links should work and open in the appropriate tabs. If you're certain that screen recordings, heat maps, or click maps are important in understanding the impact of the test, set up these elements separately.

You may have various other factors to think about, but I want to give you a sense of what's involved in prepping a test for launch. Think through the entire test experience from your user's perspective and from the lens of what information you need to show in order to prove or disprove the specific hypothesis of the test. When that's in place, you're ready to launch your test.

TIP

When you launch your test, you'll likely use one of the more popular testing tools, like Google Optimize, Optimizely, Visual Website Optimizer, or Zoho PageSense. Others are on the market, but the ones I just mentioned tend to be good starting points. Whatever tool you use, you have to install a snippet of code on your site, as with any other technology. (If you've never done this before, all tools provide you with simple step-by-step instructions to follow.)

At some point, all the prep work is done and you can finally start testing. The testing tool interfaces are all similar in that you pick the kind of test you want to run (I tell you more about this in the next section), select the page you want to test, and create a variant based on that page where you directly change the element(s) you're testing within the visual editor of the testing tool. This bit about being able to create variants on your own isn't obvious when you first use such a tool, but it makes a lot of sense because it eliminates the need for any engineering resource to create variants and be more agile about testing. Lastly, you pick the goals of the test (more sign-ups, for example, or more clicks or more orders), which are based on the hypothesis you're testing, and then start the test.

REMEMBER

These tools all have similar reporting capabilities as well, where you get to see the progress of the test over time. Though it's tempting to view the progress daily and get excited about which variants are performing well, you should avoid doing so. Check in at the end of a week's worth of running the test and make the call of whether to run the test longer. (Figure 9-2 shows a conversion rate report produced by Google Optimize.)

Testing variants

When anyone talks about testing, it's always in the context of making a change to something, then putting both versions in front of similar populations and observing the results of that change. That new version that includes the change is called a variant.

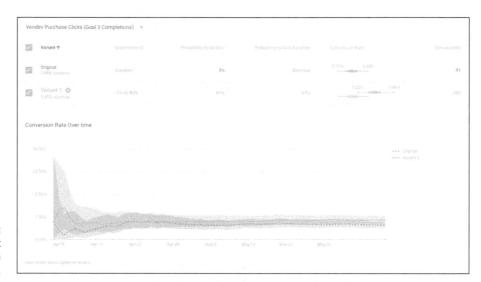

A/B tests

When people talk about testing, they're almost always referring to A/B testing, also known as *split testing.* An *A/B test* is an experiment where you randomly assign 50 percent of participants to a control group and the other half to a variant group to test the impact of the change. The variant group differs from the control in just one way so that you can attribute and measure the impact of that change. (Sounds easy in theory, but it's hard to do in practice; there are nuances that you need to consider when doing these tests, which I cover in greater detail later in this chapter.)

Even if you've never done an A/B test, you already know how the general process of how to conduct one. When you were in school and performed experiments in chemistry lab, this is what you were doing — testing to see what would happen if you added or removed variables to a control group. And just as you would do with a growth experiment, you did it in conjunction with a hypothesis that helped you understand whether the result was meaningful.

A simple example of an A/B test is where you change the tagline on your site's home page. (See Figure 9-3.) You should split traffic 50/50 traffic split between the current page and its variation.

WARNING

Unlike in a lab situation, where it's easier to control variables, when it comes to online traffic, there is inherent variability. Though you can try to minimize the impact of this variability, you'll rarely (if ever) have a perfect control for any test. This also means that you'll rarely have 100 percent certainty about the accuracy of your results.

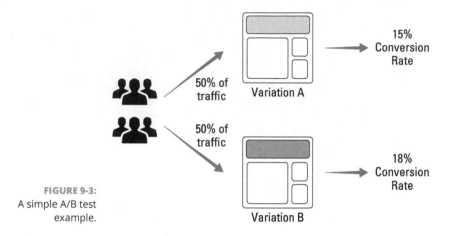

FIGURE 9-3:
A simple A/B test
example.

Just as you can do an A/B test to test two variations, you can do A/Bn tests to test
many variations of the same variable, if you have the traffic to support this,
because now you have so many more places to send the same traffic as you would
for an A/B test to be able to see a meaningful result. If you were to test four
variations, you'd have an A/B/C/D test, as shown in Figure 9-4. In this case, you'd
send 25 percent of traffic to each variant.

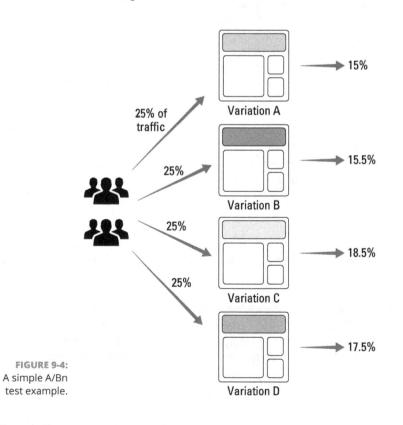

FIGURE 9-4:
A simple A/Bn
test example.

Multivariate and bandit tests

An A/B test is the most popular type of test because it's relatively easy to comprehend and execute. Tests can get more involved when you run multivariate and bandit tests.

Whereas A/B tests compare the impact of a change with one variable, multivariate tests look at what happens when you change multiple variables. With such tests, you learn more about which variable, individually or in combination, has the biggest desired impact. (See Figure 9-5.)

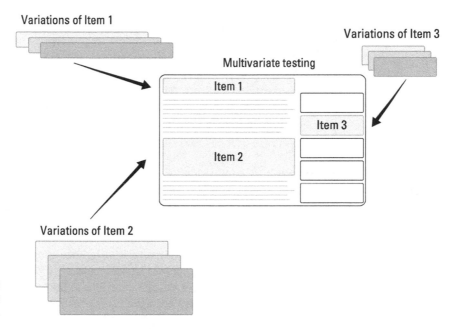

FIGURE 9-5:
A multivariate
test example.

TIP

Think about multivariate tests as a way to level up an A/B test. If the latter helps you figure out which elements on a page work best, the former helps you understand how those different elements are working together. You'll hopefully find yourself in a state where the cliché of the sum of the parts ends up being greater than the individual pieces. So always consider running both kinds of tests.

WARNING

Because you're testing more variables simultaneously, you also need more traffic, to ensure that your results are meaningful.

Bandit testing, also known as *multi-armed bandit testing* is used to describe A/Bn tests (three or more variants, in other words), where algorithms shift traffic to variations that are performing well in real-time. (Think of the proverbial slot machine player in Las Vegas, who plays a number of "one-armed bandits" at a time in order to optimize the payout.)

This is different from a normal A/Bn test, where you'd pick a winner only after analyzing the data. So, a huge benefit of bandit testing is that it mitigates the opportunity cost of A/B testing — the conversions lost during the duration of a test with a worse-performing variation, in other words. (See Figure 9-6.) However, as with multi-variate testing, you need to conduct a lot of traffic for these tests to provide meaningful results.

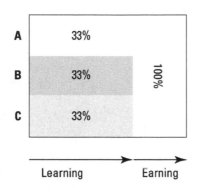
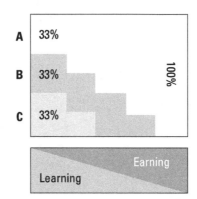

FIGURE 9-6:
A bandit testing illustration.

WARNING

A huge constraint in running bandit tests is the fact that they're algorithm based. By definition, they're more complicated to execute. So be careful about running such tests in specific scenarios, where the return is proportional to the resource investment.

TIP

Pages or page elements that are short-lived — holiday campaigns or those based around specific events, for example — are good places to consider for such tests. You could be testing pages, sites, or just headlines. You don't have the luxury of waiting for an A/Bn test to end to see which test performs best.

Other scenarios where bandit testing makes a lot of sense include those where you might have to continually optimize (and, by extension, even retest) specific elements over time, like on an e-commerce site. The cost of manually running and analyzing such tests over the long-term can be outweighed by a bandit testing approach, which also provides a level of automation to the analysis and optimization part.

REMEMBER

Whatever type of tests you run, as long you systematically pick the tests you run and learn from them, your odds of success increase. Having said that, when you're first starting out, setting yourself a goal of getting proficient with A/B (or (A/Bn) testing first, is a good starting point before attempting the more complex types of tests.

REMEMBER

Although I've been talking about testing from the perspective of doing it within the product for most of this chapter, I don't want you to think that means testing within acquisition channels isn't as important. You will have to do this at some point if you're going to grow the number of people who use your product meaningfully. It's just that I think of acquisition tests in the same way as product tests because the process remains the same. You should be testing different channels for results that show where more of your potential customers may already be. You'll be testing everything from content to ads. As with product tests, test big things first, whether its different content or content formats or writing styles, to find what resonates with your ideal audience. When you find a positive test result, optimize with smaller changes.

Common testing pitfalls and ways to work around them

It's a fact of life that you need to have a hypothesis before you test an idea. Ignore this basic fact at your peril, because you really shouldn't be testing anything without this basic consideration. Beyond this, though, are some common pitfalls that you'll likely encounter when starting out.

Refusing to work with minimal viable tests

I know from personal experience how easy it is to get caught up with wanting to design the perfect test. I also know what it's like to fall into the trap of believing, "We need XYZ to be able to run this test." With minimum viable tests, the idea is to find the cheapest, fastest way to get data so that you can make a call, one way or another.

In practice, this can mean using tools for a purpose other than their original intent (a survey tool as a lead capture form, for example) or creating landing pages and/ or buttons that go nowhere so that you can gauge interest with clicks. (This is a practice called smoke tests that can save you time and resources for building something before validating the need for it.) No matter how things ends up, just remember that the test is not about the results per se, but rather about what you're trying to learn. Keeping that point in mind helps free you up to think about alternative ways to achieve the same outcomes versus being trapped by what you know.

Not testing to statistical significance

When you're testing, the biggest problem is understanding whether the impact of tests is caused by chance or by the changes you made. This is problematic, of course, because it has a true business impact.

Before beginning a test, assume a *null hypothesis* — the contention that the differences between the variations will have no impact on conversions. In other words, assume that any variation in conversions is based on pure chance. Your test, then, is to disprove this null hypothesis. That means you cannot base your decisions purely on the observed results of a single run of a test; rather, you have to produce a statistically significant pool of results in order to come to a valid conclusion.

TIP

To obtain statistical significance, the test needs to be to run with an appropriate sample size and for a sufficient period that the null hypothesis is statistically disproven. Figuring out an appropriate sample size is often tricky, but you can use the easy, online sample-size calculator created by Optimizely: www.optimizely. com/sample-size-calculator. Another option is the Visual Website Optimizer calculator, which relies on a few more questions: https://vwo.com/tools/ ab-test-duration-calculator). Finally, the simple Unbounce calculator gives you both a sample size and a recommended duration: https://unbounce.com/ ab-test-duration-calculator). Whichever calculator you choose, stick with one so that you're consistent in your decision-making.

TIP

If you input high traffic numbers, these calculators may indicate that you need only a few days to reach statistical significance. Always test for at least a week, even in such cases, because every day has its own variation. Many practitioners recommend testing for a minimum of two weeks, no matter what. Either way, you need to ensure that you've tested to account for all inherent variability. Similarly, you also need to account for seasonality. If certain times of the year naturally have higher traffic (like the holiday shopping season), repeat the tests during nonpeak times, to confirm that the results still hold.

TIP

If you don't have high traffic yet or you're testing on a high-value but low-traffic page, you don't have a sufficient sample size. A common rule of thumb that we followed at GrowthHackers was to wait until we had recorded between 250 and 300 conversions per variation in this case.

If you have very little traffic or even lower conversion rates as a natural course of your business, testing may take months to show results. Don't bother testing in this case. Make the (big) change and see what happens.

Lastly, when talking about statistical significance, "everyone" generally means "at least 95 percent significance." This is just a generally accepted convention in statistics for confidence in testing results.

TIP

The exception to the rule that we followed at GrowthHackers was in running initial tests. These were big changes or things we'd never tried. In this case, we were looking more for whether we saw any signal that might be worth our time and effort to pursue with further optimization tests. We weren't evaluating these initial tests from the lens of significance as much as for potential business impact.

Not understanding the change correctly

A common confusion when analyzing tests is to conflate the difference in conversions between variations — say, 10 percent versus 15 percent — and the percentage increase in conversion rate from 10 percent to 15 percent. Both descriptions say something different about the results. When you don't understand this difference, you can make the wrong decision on which version to implement.

Running overlapping tests

Running overlapping tests happens more often than most testers care to admit. The trick is to minimize how often this happens. In the interest of speed, you might be tempted to run more than one test at the same time — say, on the home page and on your checkout page, where both tests have similar impact (increasing sales, for example).

How do you know whether the increase in sales was due to the home page change, the checkout page change, or both? One solution is to run multivariate tests, as I describe earlier in this chapter. In this case, you also want to ensure that you evenly split traffic from each upstream variation (the home page, for example) to the ones downstream (the checkout page, for example). The other solution is to run multipage tests, where you consider a specific flow as a whole and then create variations within that flow. This strategy helps attribute results correctly.

Underestimating the shock of the new

If you change a high-traffic area of your site, returning visitors might be thrown off at first because you've changed their workflow. This could cause them to interact differently (less or more), making you form incorrect assumptions about the impact of this change.

To keep this from happening, always segment your visitors into new and returning visitors and compare their behaviors over time to judge whether it truly is the novelty effect in play, because returning visitors will adjust their behavior over time.

Not caring about small wins

Most of your testing wins over time will be smaller wins. Even if you start from scratch with a terrible site, your early big wins will taper out and you'll end up with small wins — when you get them. Depending on your product, small wins may mean a lot. But even if it doesn't, these wins will compound over time. At the moment, the numbers may seem small, but when you look back on them, you'll see how they all added up. Bottom line: Don't think that you don't have opportunities to test further, even in areas with small wins (depending on the relative priority of other tests in your backlog).

Not sticking with it

You're never running tests in a vacuum. Objectives inform where you test, and tests fail regularly. This doesn't mean that, just because you tested a specific hypothesis and the test didn't work, you necessarily have to look for totally different areas in which to test. All you learned is that a specific hypothesis didn't bear out. If you believe that your testing objective is correct, thar's gold to be found there. Figure out why your test failed, and then test again with a refined hypothesis based on the insights gained.

Not running tests repeatedly

Sean Ellis made it a point at GrowthHackers to ensure that our growth team was always testing and learning, and a large backlog of ideas was the key to ensuring that they had something to test. His bigger point, though, was that if you weren't learning fast about what worked and what didn't, you were missing out on opportunities to grow the business faster.

The other concept that became obvious quickly was that testing is a habit, and habits can be broken. And once they break, they can be hard to get back. (Have you ever tried going back to the gym after a long break?)

Analyzing Results

Analyzing results is the most important part of testing — the learning part. Learning is a function of looking at your data correctly, and that almost always is a function of segmenting it to look at it from different perspectives for insights. These insights will come from manipulating data in your various analytics tools, whether it's Google Analytics and/or a behavioral analytics tool.

The first question you have to answer is, "Did this test win?" In trying to answer it, you'll find that either none of the variations beats the control (none disproved the null hypothesis, in other words) or that one or more of the variations did in fact beat the control (in a significant manner). Every now and then, the results are inconclusive either way.

TIP

Ensure that your team is clear on the meaning of the terms *winning*, *losing*, and *inconclusive* in this context:

>> **Won:** At least one tested variant showed a statistically significant positive improvement for the primary goal (and other goals, as applicable) over the original.

>> **Lost:** All tested variants showed statistically significant negative differences for the primary goal (and other goals, as applicable) compared to the original.

>> **Inconclusive:** All tested variants showed about the same performance — no statistically significant positive or negative improvement for the primary goal (and other goals, as applicable) over the original, in other words.

After you've verified that the sample size, duration, significance (if it matters for this test), and other factors all check out, you implement that test fully within your product and evaluate its real-world impact.

Before you take that step with your winners, though, investigate the various segments impacted by this test, such as the common ones in this list:

>> Organic traffic versus paid traffic versus referral traffic

>> New visitors versus returning visitors

>> Mobile visitors versus desktop visitors

>> Visitors from different browsers, operating systems, and device types

>> Home page visitors versus visitors who start on specific pages

>> Hour of the day or day of the week

>> Location of visitors

>> Logged-in users versus logged-out users

Differences in behavior between segments gives you insights into where you might focus future tests for even greater impact. Everything is of interest here, from how a segment flowed through pages of interest to how long they stayed and every other interaction point until they reached the end point (or not). This segmentation also helps you arrive at the right conclusion. The reason is that at times you may find that, on an overall basis, a variation may not beat the control — though for specific segments they might, which might lead you to a completely different conclusion.

TIP

If there's no difference between variations in all cases, there may be an issue with your implementation — everything from how you interpreted your research for the test to how you set up your measurements for the test. That's why it can be helpful to retrace your steps, to understand why you're seeing this lack of difference across the board.

REMEMBER

The type of business should also inform how you analyze your result. For an e-commerce site, you might be more interested in how new-versus-returning visitors behave or how emails impact existing customers. This is different from a B2B SaaS where the quality of leads and the entire buying journey may take on a more important role.

WARNING

Avoid analysis paralysis. Segmentation can be a never-ending rabbit hole. To help calibrate the amount of time you spend on analysis, think about the impact of this test on your objective metrics and your North Star Metric. If the impact is expected to be large, spend more time. If not, don't. You'll be better off spending less time on analyzing lower-impact tests and running more tests instead.

If testing does anything to you, it infuses you with a healthy dose of paranoia. (I know that's what testing does to me.) If you made a change, you'll expect to see an impact. But what about the impacts you never anticipated?

I find it helpful to pull back from the immediate test and ask myself what else might I expect people to do after they've interacted with my product or a specific element on my site. This helps you to look beyond the immediate "transaction" of the test and see whether the win you're claiming is coming at the cost of another element downstream. The only way I've found to find patterns for how to analyze follow-on effects is to just analyze more tests. No silver bullets here, either, my friend.

Ultimately, you want to understand the Why — why did one variant win, and what can you learn about your users and customers based on this? When you do understand the Why, you're better able to come up with more ideas and hypotheses to test. It also helps you reprioritize tests based on this new information.

REMEMBER

As you analyze your tests and record your results and the insights you've gained, don't forget to include other important information about your test. This includes the experiment dates, information about the audience, links to the experiment itself, screen shots as objective evidence, and any other information that's pertinent to the results (whether the test was part of a larger holiday campaign, for example).

Acting on What You've Learned

You'll soon find out that taking what you've learned and running with it is the most fun part of the testing process, because irrespective of how a test may have performed, you now have more information to make better decisions about how to grow the business. This is nothing but a loop you'll keep going through as part of the growth process. (See Figure 9-7.)

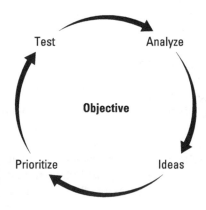

FIGURE 9-7: The growth process loop.

If a test won, you also have to figure out how to make that change a permanent part of your product or process. If a test lost or was inconclusive, it's an opportunity to revise your thinking with new data and try again.

I lay out some ways to think about what to do next based on each of these scenarios.

Winning tests

I am assuming that if you've followed the growth process and involved the right people upfront, you won't encounter scenarios where you have to consider implementing winning tests that don't help move your NSM and don't negatively impact your brand and customer experience. This may seem like an odd thing to say but it can be tempting to not think about your NSM just because you saw a big change to some number someone higher up in the organization cares about from a test. At other times, making changes that provide a terrible experience to the customer but moves some other metric you care about in a big way can sway your thinking to just keep doing more of that to show the higher-ups regularly what a big impact the testing program is making. Short-term wins, whether they involve conversions or revenue, are never worth it. If you do find yourself in such a situation, initiate a discussion between key stakeholders regarding how such a test ended up being run in the first place, and look for opportunities to improve the prioritization and nomination process to mitigate for such scenarios.

When you achieve your first wins, they'll likely involve situations where you have one winning variation as a result of an A/B test. The most common course of action would be to make this variation available to 100 percent of your visitors, users, or customers. Irrespective of which testing tool you use, you can do this quite easily from within the tool you're using.

But this isn't the end of this implementation. If the winning variation was a combination of steps, you have to document this process. If it was the result of a change on the site or in the product, you have to ensure that this change is made permanently within that environment.

This is where you start to realize the benefit of including the key engineering and product stakeholders as part of your growth meeting. Because these people were there when this test was agreed on, and when the results were discussed, they won't be caught off guard by this request to add the task of making the test variant permanent.

The key stakeholders will (or should) have already built in a buffer to accommodate these requests within their own planning workflows so that the changes can quickly be made permanent. Be aware, however, that a time lag will occur when these changes become truly permanent. This is why having the ability to let everyone experience the winning variation directly from your testing tool is so important. It mimics the final environment until your team can move the change through its workflow.

WARNING

The alignment between engineering, product, and growth teams is of supreme importance. Nailing it down requires upfront agreements for action, which may require multiple meetings and planning outside of the context of growth meetings. This has to be done to be able to take advantage of the insights gained from your tests in order to rapidly grow the value you provide your customers. For this to work, the entire process must be built on a culture of trust and faith that such changes are nontrivial and are being made in the interest of growing value to your customers.

When I see winning tests, I like to think about next actions in terms of increasing breadth, depth, or efficiency. Here are a few ideas for what to do next based on such wins:

>> **Breadth:** Wins with messaging, copy changes, images, and video tests should naturally inspire you to ask where else you can try the same thing. Made a change to the home page image? Try it in an ad. Tried new copy on the home page? Try putting it in another part of the site that plays an important part in converting people. Then expand that testing by exposing different types of user segments to such tests to see whether you can increase the number of people who engage with such changes. The options are endless, but you need to think about how you can expand the reach of such wins.

>> **Depth:** Say you started adding reviews to your site and this decision led to more orders. Now you know that people need to see something else to be able to trust your product before they buy. Try providing even more proof, such as adding product pictures to reviews, showing the same product picture from different angles, posting video testimonials, or even featuring case studies. Whatever it is, give people more of what they need to see in order to increase their level of engagement with these changes and its impact on your goals.

>> **Frequency:** Say you tried a test that involved promoting a piece of content and you saw an uptick in sign-ups for your trial. A possible follow-up test would be to test promoting it on more than one day, or more than once a day, to see whether simply exposing your audience to the same content multiple times has a measurable impact. Similarly, tests that increase how often users engage with your product to derive value — say, by receiving progress notifications — may tell you something about the ideal usage frequency of your product and inform your thinking about tests that have to do what should be in those notifications and when to send them.

>> **Efficiency:** Say you have more than one winning variation — perhaps one includes an image and another one has fewer form fields. Your next step should be to combine these wins into a single variant and test it against others, where you play around with other elements, whether it involves adding more information or pre-filling information, for example. Think of the ideal results of such tests fitting the old cliché "The sum is greater than the parts." Such tests, where you mix and match winning ideas like this, can help you understand more about how fast you can help people derive value from your product.

TIP

If a delay occurs in creating the new variant that combines winning elements, you have a few choices based on your analysis. If the variant with the biggest overall impact is also the one with the biggest impact to your most valuable customer segment, just switch to that one for now. If a variant that did not have the biggest overall impact had the best response with your most valuable customer segment, consider creating a personalized experience for this segment while you prepare the combined test to launch. Every testing tool allows you create a personalized experience based on the results of tests for any audience characteristics you specify.

Whichever path you take with your winning test, remember that a follow-up test is not guaranteed to be a win. Some tests may start to show diminishing returns as you try to optimize them even further, with some performing worse much faster than others.

One clear example at GrowthHackers occurred when we posted community submissions to Twitter for impact on traffic back to the site. We found that we could turn up the frequency of posting updates every ten minutes because we had so much content to post, and it had minimal negative impact. When we turned up the rate to every five minutes, we found that people started to click less because our updates were overwhelming their feeds. It also had a negative impact on clicking through from our weekly round-up emails because now more people had already seen (more) content on Twitter, so they no longer needed to see what they had missed in the email. The rate was pulled back to ten minutes, and everything else then corrected itself.

Losing tests

Some people think that losing tests are bad and that you should try to mitigate their number. The reality is that most tests don't win. I've seen this personally and heard it from other practitioners. The other truth is that losing tests aren't failures — they're learning opportunities that should be embraced because they tell you more about what not to do and where you might want to focus moving forward. Anything that helps you learn more about how to provide more value to your customers should be welcomed with open arms.

Just as you asked, "Why did this test win?" when analyzing your losing variants to understand next steps, you also need to ask, "Why did this test lose?" In many ways, you're doing the reverse of what you did when analyzing your winning variants — the idea now is to understand factors such as which segments converted worse than others.

The important thing is to see whether you can frame your understanding of what happened in the form of an alternative hypothesis about how to create a positive impact. Sometimes, that insight may just be that the change was too small to matter and you need to test a bolder hypothesis. Whatever the case may be, you have two options based on your analysis:

>> **Try a completely different strategy.** Sometimes, and especially as you've already extracted wins from a specific line of testing over time, you'll find that there are no more (meaningful) gains to be had. It's important to recognize when this is happening, because it's the trigger to reevaluate not only whether you need to try something different in terms of testing but also whether you're approaching the end of your ability to impact your objective metrics and need to move on to a new focus area.

Also, the opportunity cost of testing will start to outweigh any gains you might see from making minor tweaks — another sign that it is time to move on.

>> **Try a sort-of different strategy.** The fact that you see a negative result tells you that the change you made affected people's behavior. If you're not yet at the point where you need to move on to a different strategy, think about alternative ways to conduct the same test. Sometimes, it's simply a question of execution or how people experience a test that makes them react negatively to it.

Say you tried a certain type of image on your home page and it reduced sign-ups — maybe you just need to try another kind of image or move the image to another location or replace it with a GIF version. You get the idea.

Inconclusive tests

If you've constructed your tests correctly with a good hypothesis and measurement, such results should be in the minority. Assuming you've taken care of the basics, the main reason that tests are inconclusive is that they're taking longer than expected to provide a significant result.

You're always having to weigh the benefit of waiting for more data versus the need to move on to the next test. If you have tests that are taking longer than most tests usually do to show you a result one way or the other, perhaps it's telling you that the changes you're testing aren't that different. Maybe you need to reconsider a more noticeable change and test it instead. That might mean testing multiple new elements at a time instead of just one at a time, or it might mean making the change so distinctive or noticeable that there has to be a strong(er) reaction to it over the original.

Systemizing changes

It should be apparent by now that as you test and learn, the insights gained should feed more ideas. This loop never stops as long as you test within a certain objective.

As you start getting winning tests, though, you have to decide how to scale them. Depending on the kind of test you're dealing with, you have two choices: Systemize the insights gained by making changes in your product, or change some processes.

When a winning test is a combination of steps, many of which aren't in your product and/or the culmination of insights gained from multiple earlier tests, you have to adapt your processes to reflect this. You can use technology to automate parts of the workflow, but often there's a manual component to replicating the impact of a test again and again as a normal part of your operation.

Take generating content as an example. You may have found that a certain type of long-form content, written for a given audience so that it can be published on your blog and then cross-promoted on two specific channels, produces the highest-quality leads for your business. Much is involved here.

You have to do keyword research, for which you use a specific tool. You create outlines; assign a writer, a timeline, and an editor; provide writing guidelines; designate assets, a publishing date, and a review process; and so on — all before you even start publishing it on the blog. How an approved post makes its way to the blog and who is responsible for it is its own workflow. After that's done, the handoff to the person(s) who promotes this content across channels, and the guidelines for frequency of promotion and for how the content is amplified, all have their own steps. Measuring the impact of the content (leads, in other words) and reporting on it also has its own checklist to follow.

Given that the process, when followed a certain way, will produce the result you want, you have to document this as a "playbook" of sorts. This playbook can be as involved as necessary for you and your team to be able to replicate the steps correctly. You can use Google Docs, with steps and screen shots, or a template in a task management tool, where you can assign owners and due dates for each step. No matter how you choose to do it, the goal is to reduce variability in the process so that you can have confidence in the outcome.

This approach ensures that you take full advantage of the insights gained from your past wins and not repeating (perhaps, incorrectly) or relearning anything unnecessary. Of course, as you execute on a process over time, you'll discover more efficiencies, and you can adapt that process as you learn more.

The biggest advantage of this approach is that, as your team grows, all these insights and processes become part of the onboarding and training for new team members, helping them to start executing much sooner.

Chapter **10**

Managing the Growth Process

Your company's North Star Metric and the growth model you develop informs your objectives and tests, but you also need a growth process in place so that you can keep on top of all the various moving pieces in a way that lets you feel confident that you're always focusing on the right things. This growth process, like all of growth hacking, is iterative, systematic, and data-informed.

Establishing a Weekly Routine

When I worked at GrowthHackers, only one recurring meeting involved all members of the growth team: the weekly growth meeting. It included the CEO, the head of growth, and the heads of all departments. All key stakeholders were expected to attend this meeting. Others were asked to attend on an as-needed basis. The growth meeting was commonly referred to as the company's "most expensive meeting" because, for an hour every week, the opportunity cost of having more than five people attending a single meeting was quite high. So, the meeting had to have a high return on investment.

Over my more than three years at GrowthHackers, the process and tools that were used evolved in order to make the weekly growth meeting more efficient. Sean Ellis was always open to new ideas from team members, making the meeting itself something that was optimized, much like our product.

REMEMBER

The growth meeting itself is just one part of what should become your regularly scheduled weekly activities. The meeting's purpose is to focus on what you've learned and the insights gained. The rest of the week is about launching tests, analyzing completed tests, and reserving time to prepare for the next week's meeting.

TIP

Host your growth meeting early in the week so that you don't lose momentum when it comes to launching tests. The GrowthHackers meeting was held on Tuesday mornings at 10 o'clock, which provided about three-and-a-half days in the remainder of the week to launch tests. Do what works for you (other companies have held them on Monday), though I recommend holding this meeting no later than Tuesday.

A typical week (see Figure 10-1) might look something like this example:

Monday: Prepare for growth meeting, including any analyses and nominations for new ideas to test.

Tuesday: Hold the growth meeting.

Wednesday–Friday: Launch tests, analyze completed tests, systematize winning tests, and come up with more ideas to test.

What A Typical Week Looks Like

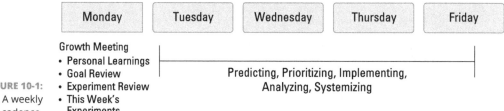

FIGURE 10-1: A weekly cadence.

Setting the Ground Rules

The growth meeting is about gaining insights (as Sean Ellis drilled into us at GrowthHackers). Its purpose is to look at the company's North Star Metric trend and objective metrics to understand why the numbers are the way they are and what needs to be done next. Every meeting has a set agenda and format to keep everyone on track and make the most of the meeting.

Before the meeting

Everyone is expected to come prepared for the growth meeting. This meeting should not be the first time you look at any piece of information, which means that you should

>> Be familiar with the current state of the North Star Metric and objective metrics

>> Know the current status of tests (ready to launch, launched, ready to analyze, or in the knowledge base)

>> Be familiar with insights gained from analyzed tests

>> Nominate an idea or two to test, based on the current objective

>> (Bonus) Contribute at least one idea to test

Here's a list of individual responsibilities:

>> **Head of growth:** The head of growth not only ensures that the entire week's activities are on track (or explains clearly why they aren't) but also updates the North Star Metric and objective metrics.

>> **Team members:** Team members can be assigned from the growth team, and sometimes from outside of it, to manage individual tests to launch. This means working with the appropriate people in engineering, design, analytics, and other departments to ensure that before the next meeting, the test is launched. The head of growth is also in the loop to help as needed.

>> **Analyst:** This person determines which tests are ready for analysis and documents the observations and conclusions to discuss during the meeting. The analyst also discusses findings with the head of growth, to ensure agreement before the growth meeting.

REMEMBER

The goal is to provide everyone involved with the growth meeting with all the information they need. You can see that a lot of documentation takes place in preparation for the meeting. Many people use Google Docs, Sheets, Trello, or a similar application for this purpose. (At GrowthHackers, we were fortunate to have our own product, called NorthStar, which was purpose-built for managing testing.) There is no right answer here — use what works for you.

Before a GrowthHackers meeting, the team was expected to familiarize themselves with the current state of metrics, tests, and learnings captured within North Star so that they could come to the meeting prepared. Team members who had insights to share were expected to add those insights to metrics or tests before joining the meeting. Fortunately for us, the tool enforced consistency by design. Whether you use a specific tool or Google Docs, be sure to provide a template for any type of update. This makes is easier to understand what the update is about to everyone on the team.

Running the meeting

The company's growth meetings should follow this agenda (at GrowthHackers, the meeting was an hour long):

15 minutes: Provide key growth metrics (North Star Metric, objectives) and issues or opportunities with each one.

10 minutes: Review the preceding week's tests (launched/not launched, in progress, analyzed, in knowledge base).

15 minutes: Discuss key lessons learned from analyzed tests.

15 minutes: Review nominations for this week's tests and finalize selection.

5 minutes: Review the growth of the idea backlog.

Right off the bat, this agenda should tell you that the growth meeting is all about gaining insights. You should continually strive to understand why things are the way they are — rather than just review what happened during the past week. If these meetings only review the week's events, they're just glorified status updates, and you won't be able to understand the impact of your efforts.

By focusing on the Why, it's easier to engage the entire team around objectives that impact your North Star Metric, because the focus is entirely on gaining insights. As the team comes to understand more about why things are the way they are, it sparks new ideas to test and questions you may never have thought to ask otherwise.

REMEMBER

Because the team includes key stakeholders from across departments, the insights gained can spread out across the organization. This strategy, which makes it easy to see their impact across all functions, shows how it makes the team's work better while involving the broader organization in the growth conversation.

To expand on what should happen during the meeting, I break down in this list the key activities during each part of the agenda:

» **15 minutes:** Key growth metrics (North Star Metric, objectives) and issues or opportunities with each one:

  a. View the trend of the North Star Metric for the current week, as well as the past three weeks to understand the cause of any upward, downward, or flat trend. (Have you had no winning tests recently, for example?)

  b. View the trend of the objective(s) for the current week as well as for the past three weeks to understand the cause of any upward, downward, or flat trend. (Has anything unusual or unexpected happened recently to impact it, for example?)

  c. Have you seen anything as a macro trend that might explain your data?

  d. Are you still focusing on the right objective(s)?

» **10 minutes:** Review last week's tests (launched/not launched, in progress, analyzed, in knowledge base).

You can see that these ten minutes are the only ones spent on the What in terms of reviewing last week's tests. But even then, you're trying to gain a better understanding of the testing process. Questions like the following are crucial:

  a. Did any tests not launch as expected? What blocked them? How can you avoid this problem in the future?

  b. Are any tests running longer than expected? If so, why is that happening? Are you testing low-traffic pages or waiting for statistical significance?

  c. Have any tests that have finished running not been analyzed yet? If so, what has caused the delay? How can you avoid this problem moving forward?

» **15 minutes:** Key lessons learned from analyzed tests.

Personally, I find the key lessons to be the most fun aspect of the growth meeting. This isn't simply a one-way conversation where the analyst shares insights gained from tests and everyone nods in agreement. This is where the rest of the team can gain greater insight into how the data is analyzed and whether the conclusions are correct. So, you're supposed to initiate an active discussion regarding how any test was run, whether the analysis was correct and sufficient, what other insights might be of interest beyond the ones that are presented, and which ideas for future tests are suggested by the results. This adds a level of rigor to the entire team's ability to learn as much as it can from each test.

REMEMBER

Producing analyses that are incomplete or completely wrong (I've had my fair share of these) can be terrifying for whoever is sharing them, but that's the point of this part of the meeting — you have to be learning the right things from our tests. So, although the focus is on gaining insights, don't forget that human beings are putting themselves on the line here. This is also why it's important for the head of growth to review these analyses before the meeting, to mitigate situations where incorrect or incomplete analyses are being viewed by the team. It's also the job of the head of growth to help encourage the analyst to be thorough and not look at any challenges to their analyses as any form of public embarrassment. Everything should be looked at from the lens of understanding what it takes to grow the North Star Metric.

The other concept to keep in mind is that sharing insights gained can be a lot of fun. You can easily get carried away by tending to the details of tests or letting those insights gained become fodder for tangential discussions. You have 15 minutes to share and discuss the insights gained, so make the most of it. The head of growth plays a role in keeping things on track (and for the whole meeting).

TIP

Every so often, you uncover a detail that leads to an amazing new insight or a big win. Don't forget to celebrate it as a team, during the meeting and after the meeting. These are rare, and their importance cannot be understated. Recognize, in front of the entire company, the person who came up with the original idea. And take any excuse for a celebratory meal with the entire growth team.

>> **15 minutes:** Review nominations for this week's tests and finalize selection.

I mention earlier in this chapter that, before the meeting begins, everyone should nominate an idea or two to test. By definition, these ideas have to map to your current objectives. Ideally, everyone nominates ideas that someone else came up with, but it's acceptable to nominate one of your own, if you feel strongly about it. This strategy helps minimize personal bias overrunning nominations. The point of nominating ideas before the meeting begins is to ensure that less time is spent deciding *during* the meeting what to even consider in the first place.

Because the GrowthHackers growth meeting was attended, on average, by half a dozen people, they produced a maximum of 12 ideas that could even be considered for testing in any given week. In some weeks, fewer than 12 ideas were considered, because some were nominated by multiple people. Of these, 3–5 ideas were given the green light to test that week. Even though the goal was to launch three tests per week, more tests could be launched as long as the time and resources were available.

This part of the meeting was the "horse trading" phase: Whoever nominated an idea had to make the case for why that idea was the best one to test that week. Every person had 30 seconds to make the case for each test they nominated. When someone made the case for an idea to be tested, team members — with their varying expertise — were responsible for asking questions to get more context as to whether the scoring applied was correct.

For example, if an idea had a high Ease score, feedback from product or engineering team members might lower that score, potentially taking it out of contention that week. Similarly, a lack of supporting data for high Impact scores led to a lowering of those scores. Ideas that had no hypotheses or ICE scores associated with them weren't considered. The person nominating an idea had to work with the originator of the idea to ensure that it had enough information in it to allow the rest of the team to decide on it. (For more on scoring protocols, including discussions of Ease scores, Impact scores, and ICE scores, check out Chapter 8.)

>> **5 minutes:** Review the growth of the idea backlog.

You might think that this part of the meeting is disposable. After all, how hard is it to see how many new ideas were submitted last week? In fact, these five minutes provide an opportunity to end on a high note.

When the growth team is repeatedly contributing ideas, that's quite helpful. You always want more ideas in your backlog than you can ever test. (When I left GrowthHackers, it had more than 1,500 untested ideas!) What's even better, however, is seeing a trend showing that idea generation is consistent or growing over time, especially when ideas originate from outside the growth team.

This, then, leads to an opportunity to recognize your top idea generators. Most ideas generally come from within the growth team, but if an outsider is among your top idea contributors, you should celebrate that fact during and after the meeting.

On the flip side, if you're seeing a lack of participation from growth team members (and even the organization as a whole), acknowledge it and commit to doing better next week.

REMEMBER

The process of testing and learning is a habit. Ensure that the growth meeting happens consistently at the same time and follows the same format. You must work at it because it's hard work to keep it going week after week.

The growth meeting is a big part of building a culture of growth at your company. As with anything that has to do with culture, you should reward the right behaviors and nip the bad ones in the bud. Encourage all behaviors that contribute to greater learning and efficiency. Brian Balfour, the former vice president of growth at HubSpot, often said, "Be the best at getting better." This principle is useful for the entire team to internalize. If someone's behavior is holding back how you and your team learn about growth efficiently, however, you need to address that behavior so that you don't send mixed messages about acceptable conduct.

Here are a couple more of my thoughts about growth meetings:

>> **Ramp up slowly.** When you're starting out, the format of the growth meeting is a bit different from the agenda you'll end up with. The attendees are different, too.

Sean Ellis often said, early on, that the CEO is the de facto head of growth. So, when starting out, it's easier for the CEO to start working with someone who has great project management skills. The CEO identifies the North Star Metric and the growth objectives that need to be achieved. The CEO then works with the Project Manager (PM) to identify tests to launch. The PM is empowered to work on an ad hoc basis with whoever is vital to launching tests as needed. The CEO and the PM then work together to analyze tests and extract insights from them in a dedicated growth meeting that is likely shorter than a full-fledged growth meeting. These two people are also likely to be the only two contributors to ideas for a while (until you get comfortable with the process of testing and learning weekly).

REMEMBER

When you're just starting out and you're trying to build the habit of testing, don't make the effort too difficult for yourself. Start with the goal of getting a single test launched every week. It may help to start with "easy" tests that you can do on your own — changes in website copy, for example, or email subject lines — to learn how to construct a test properly with the right hypotheses and to analyze them correctly.

As you become more comfortable running one test every week, add another one and then another, with the initial goal of launching at least three tests per week. When you do this, you start to encounter things that get in the way of launching tests. This is likely because, as you run out of "easy" tests that you can do on your own, you'll need more help from others to launch tests. Because everyone else's help is on an ad hoc basis at this stage, their priorities almost always overtake yours. This is beneficial because, if the reason your tests don't get launched is that you lack a person with the necessary skills, that helps the CEO make the case for whether that resource needs to be reassigned (partially, to start) or whether it's time to add a full-time hire to fulfil that need. This might be a creative person, an engineer, a formal growth lead, or a data analyst, depending on what the need is. You'll inevitably add more dedicated growth roles as you continue testing.

>> **Keep the habit.** Missing even a single growth meeting can be a momentum killer. When the entire GrowthHackers site was being rebuilt from the ground up and no tests could be run on the site for three weeks as a result, there was a lot of confusion until it was restarted — some employees had even forgotten how to prepare and participate in growth meetings. Another week passed before everyone was back on track and could regain their momentum.

If tests were run temporarily outside the site — on, say, acquisition channels — at least the momentum would have continued, even if the tests didn't map to the company's objectives. The *habit* is the more important part. Even if it means that you're in a situation where you can run only "meaningless" tests, like changing button colors or positions of images — even without a valid hypothesis — do it! Maintaining the habit with "bad" tests is more important than waiting to run good tests. And, who knows? Sometimes, the tests that you never would have considered otherwise may just give you ideas for additional tests. Don't underestimate the power of serendipity in lighting unexpected paths to growth.

Moving to a Month-to-Month Schedule

Make no mistake: Keeping up a weekly cadence of testing is hard and takes a lot of discipline. It's also easy to get caught up in the feeling that you're doing "a lot of testing," because you maintain that high tempo week after week. If you don't build in a system of repeatedly checking in to figure out what your tests are accomplishing, you may find yourself on a wheel of meaningless testing, which can quickly lead you into a downward spiral that ends in your not running any tests because you don't see the point of it all. I walk you through two mandatory activities to help you avoid this trap, which also help continue the momentum of testing month over month.

Reviewing objectives monthly

I talk in Chapter 7 about the superpower of developing objectives when it comes to keeping your testing on track to impact your North Star positively. I also mention keeping your focus on an objective for at least 30 days, a time frame that gives your tests enough time to show meaningful impact.

Think about it: When you're first starting out, you may not be running more than one or two tests a week. That's just four to eight tests a month — and some of them may not even work. That means the signal you're getting is quite small, though you need to give yourself enough time to see it. Also, just because you launched a test in a given week doesn't necessarily mean that it will be ready to analyze the following week. The fact is, you may need at least seven to ten days before you can understand the impact of any test. The same dynamic applies even when you have a more mature testing program. The metrics you'll focus on will naturally have a higher bar than when you first started out. So it's imperative that your team have the space to understand whether the current testing focus is working. And again, the 30-day mark is a great point at which to reevaluate whether there's a meaningful signal to continue the current testing focus.

A common characteristic of testing when you're first starting out is that you'll most likely experience a lot of failed tests, because you have little information about what works and what doesn't. As you collect more data, your win rate should start to improve.

While you're evaluating the impact of your testing focus, keep an eye on how well you're doing when it comes to achieving the objectives you've set. If you find yourself almost always crushing your objective metrics, you're likely not being aggressive with them and will need to reevaluate how far you can go. As you set newer objectives (or continue existing ones), also test your team's ability to hit more ambitious goals with these objectives.

TIP

At GrowthHackers, we set a confidence level for objectives based on data we had. To avoid getting bogged down in specifics, we determined whether we had a less than, equal to, or greater than a 50-50 shot at achieving our objectives. This way, if we could see that even if we had very low odds of hitting our goals and we kept meeting or beating them, we could be bolder with our goals moving forward.

We also paired this with an official goal and an unofficial goal to make it fun for everyone. The official goal was one that, if we kept hitting it, we needed to be more aggressive. The unofficial goal was our super-ambitious goal — if we hit it, we knew we were on to something big. As with individual tests, the odds of scoring one of these kinds of wins is rare — maybe once a year — but we absolutely wanted to know when we did this, because it's definitely a cause for celebration. That is not to say that any result between these two goals wasn't something we'd be proud of achieving. The point was to always know when to revise goals and when to know that we had just hit something big.

REMEMBER

The same logic you use with your official goals also applies to the unofficial goals. If you're hitting these more than once or twice a year, get even more aggressive with them.

SWAP MEETINGS

Anyone in charge of growth will run through a version of the meeting structure I lay out in the "Setting the Ground Rules" section, earlier in this chapter. This means that everyone has likely tweaked the process to meet their own needs. In the spirit of iteration and learning, you should learn from other growth leaders, to see how you can improve your own process: For example, swap the responsibility of leading growth meetings with someone from a different company. If you do this exercise with someone you trust and admire, you'll find blind spots revealed in your thinking that you wouldn't notice without the help of someone coming in with a different perspective.

You'll even benefit when this person is in a different kind of business or has a different business model. At the end of the day, growth is about understanding the system that generates value for your customers, makes money for the business as a consequence, and uses the biggest levers the business can pull to accelerate these outcomes. How someone in B2B does this as compared to someone in a B2C company is different, meaning that they can offer interesting perspectives to consider.

Without a doubt, this strategy requires a lot of trust and vulnerability from both parties because you're sharing company data with an outsider. The upside, however, of having a dispassionate analysis of how you manage growth from a trusted and skilled third party is invaluable in comparison. So, your first course of business is to get your respective leadership teams on board with the benefits of this activity. They need to understand that, no matter how good your process, no one is perfect or knows everything. Having an external and trusted third-party perspective on your growth process as well as this third party's views on appropriate technology, team structure, and mindset are incredibly valuable as you work to evolve your approach to growth.

For this growth meeting to be successful, you need to set aside time beforehand to share relevant data, and they need to offer constructive feedback. They need to know the North Star Metric, the business model, your customer journey, the growth model, current objectives, tests and associated metrics, and the structure of your growth meeting. You can share this information in a Word document, in Google Docs, as a slide deck, or in any other format that works for you. This document leads to more questions about, and clarifications on, the data you've shared. But before you discuss this, have them come in and attend a growth meeting, to see how you do it, so that they can see how all of this comes together in reality for you.

Their feedback, then, should first come in written form as a response document. This saves time when you meet to discuss what isn't clear yet. Set up a meeting for this task. Block out as much time as you need to discuss their feedback. During this meeting,

(continued)

(continued)

you'll also need to agree on what the new objective might be. It might be something you were going to do anyway, but it's a useful exercise to watch someone else justify why that objective is the right one.

Be prepared for these discussions to turn into spirited debates about how and why you do what you do, because *everything* will be questioned. Long-held beliefs will be challenged. Be open to this process because, sometimes, when you've been doing things the same way for a while, you do them just because you've always done them that way, not because there's a good reason (any more) for them. Celebrate when you come across outdated "company lore." You may also end up brainstorming ideas and tactics during this time. You should capture everything in your testing backlog.

After you agree on the new objective, inform your growth team about the point of this exercise and prepare them for someone else to come in and run your next growth meeting. (The idea here is that they should be prepared to treat the new meeting leader the same way they treat you when you're running it.) When they're done with the meeting, debrief to understand what went well and what didn't. You'll also find that such debriefs often veer into the direction of coordinating cross-functional work across departments and stakeholders. If that doesn't happen, bring it up intentionally in order to understand how they manage that challenge and what you can learn. It's also a great bonding exercise to learn that you're not the only one facing this issue.

When you're done, it's your turn to pay it back and repeat the exercise of providing feedback on their growth process and running their growth meeting.

The best part of this exercise is that, irrespective of whether you're providing feedback or receiving it, you'll break out of familiar patterns and learn to think a bit differently about your approach to growth, which in itself sparks new ways of working and new ideas to test.

As you undergo this process of constantly reevaluating your objectives, your team gains increasing confidence about whether you're working on the right tasks at the right time. This in turn will impact the speed and urgency with which you tackle growth activities. It also increases the rate of learning about what works and what doesn't.

Checking on the impact of individual tests

As you test more and rack up more wins, it becomes important to understand whether the gains from those tests still hold. The sad reality is that no test is impactful forever — its impact diminishes over time. This is especially true of gains within acquisition channels, given that they keep changing, but it's also true of individual optimizations throughout the customer journey. So, if a certain sign-up test resulted in an increase of ten sign-ups per week, or if a Facebook ad results in five purchases per day, for example, are they still mostly performing that way?

Someone on your growth team should have the responsibility of repeatedly going back to review whether (and how much) you can still count on individual gains from tests. This is a time intensive process, but one you should engage in it so that you can more quickly come up with newer ideas to make up for any losses you start to see.

You can do a few things here to prevent getting bogged down with this exercise — keep in mind that you also have your ongoing growth activities to take care of! First, whenever a test is analyzed, if the expected impact was equal to or greater than 50 percent of the hypothesized impact, tag this test in a way that you can later recognize it as such a test. This way, you can prioritize your review in order to concentrate first on the tests that had the biggest impact on your growth. Second, when you're reviewing these tests, filter them by the part of the customer journey or AARRR funnel you're now focusing on. You may find opportunities to tweak (or even change) your current objectives based on what you see here. Then review the remaining high-impact tests from other parts of the customer journey, starting with acquisitions. (The deeper in the funnel you go, the longer life the impact that any one test will have.) So, you should absolutely identify the tests that have a shorter life span as opposed to others. Lastly, review the remaining tests that are left over, starting with the ones that were run first and moving up to the most recent date.

TIP

Set aside a specific day every month for this review — it helps to create a recurring calendar reminder. For the first time you conduct a review, leave aside half a day and gauge how long it really takes. When you first do it, you scramble to find current data, and it takes longer than you like. As you find the places you need to go to find current data for any test, make a note of that procedure within a Data Review section of the experiment document and date it. Then you (or anyone else tasked with this process) won't have to endure the same pain the next time. As you become more familiar with this process, you can even split up reviews between multiple team members to complete the process faster.

Taking the Long-Term Perspective

After a few rounds of optimizing your tests and objectives, you'll have information to help you evaluate the health of your entire growth process. This is an exercise you should do every quarter, or at least every six months. The health of your growth process is a function of how many tests you launch week after week, your learning rate, your win rate, and how well you enable your team for success. (Figure 10-2 shows a model for a quarterly review.)

Macro Optimization
Quarterly Review

1 Batting AVG	*How many successes to failures? Is it improving over time?*
2 Accuracy	*Are your hypotheses getting more accurate?*
3 Throughput	*How many experiments are you running in a given time period? How do you do more?*

FIGURE 10-2:
A quarterly
review.

The first thing you should be able to tell is whether you've been able to run more tests over time. If you've been able to do this, it also means that you've been able to generate more ideas as a team. Look at who's been generating the most ideas and who's barely contributing. Talk to the team (and the entire company, really) about what it takes to get more people and more ideas in the system if contributions are skewed toward a handful of people.

As you run more tests, you'll gain more insights and collect more data. As your learning rate increases, your hypotheses for follow-on tests should become more accurate. A simple way to know that this is happening is to look at how much supporting information you can provide to your hypothesis. This, in turn, informs your Confidence score, which should be higher than the prior test.

REMEMBER

During the start of your testing, you'll likely experience more failed tests than wins, but your win rate should improve. It's important to look at that win rate across multiple rounds of testing, especially when you've changed the objective. If that's not happening, it could be an indication of your not having set clear objectives, your hypotheses not being properly defined, or your analyses needing to improve. Your goal should be to increase your win rate over time, because your ability to grow your business is a direct result of this.

One thing that should become apparent as you conduct your review is that you'll come across situations or things that prevent you from improving on the execution of your growth process.

TIP

As you grow comfortable with testing, you may find that someone isn't great at project-managing individual tests and shouldn't be part of the core growth team. Conversely, you may find that someone is so good that they need to level up their skills and take on more responsibility. Or, maybe you need to add as a dedicated resource a member who was previously a shared resource, because of the increased demands of testing. So, part of this exercise is also being open to optimizing your team's capabilities on an ongoing basis.

Another common scenario is to find that you need more tools and technology to develop better insights and reporting as you run more tests and discover new opportunities. If you've been able to show the impact of your testing on your North Star Metric, you should have no problem justifying the cost of new or more technology.

Lastly, let me reiterate something I mention in the earlier "Swap meetings" sidebar. The processes mentioned in this chapter aren't set in stone — they're just a starting point. You'll most likely have to modify parts of them to suit your own needs, whether it's how you run your weekly meetings or your monthly and quarterly reviews. Do what works for you, as long as you always have in mind that the changes you're making are in the service of increasing the value you can deliver to your customers.

Chapter **11**

Laying the Right Foundation for Company-Wide Growth

My argument for growth has always been that what really moves the needle on it is when everyone in the company is aligned around what they need to do, collectively speaking, to impact their North Star Metric.

Adopting this kind of culture doesn't happen magically. It starts small, collecting data on what kind of impact the innovations that are introduced actually have on growth. As the results of testing show success, that tends to generate more support company-wide, which in turn leads to higher-level investments of support, talent, and resources.

If you've ever watched the movie *Moneyball*, the entire premise of Billy Beane's theory of baseball success is that you don't need to hit home runs to win. If you put yourself in a position to just keep hitting singles, you'll beat the team trying to chase the home runs, because the odds of hitting singles are higher.

Testing is just like that: Hit a lot of singles and score a lot of small wins, and soon the wins will pile up into something you can't ignore. Of course, you want to hit the home run too, but you take it when you get it — it's not the goal from the outset, in other words. Just as not every start-up becomes a billion-dollar company and not every post on social media can go viral, not every test will be a (big) winner.

The best way to give yourself room to build the habit of testing is to start small and simple. If you try to do big things out of the gate, you'll run into obstacles that stand in the way of just getting started, or you may even break something you shouldn't and have others question the value of what you're trying to do.

Taking Baby Steps

Building the habit of testing is more important initially than choosing an item to test. At first, when you're testing "easy" items, these will by definition be small changes. Small changes lead to small results, but you also give yourself the space to learn in relative obscurity. Here, you're doing things like testing different email headlines or the time of day that a notification is sent. Maybe you're changing a headline or a call to action or adding an image or removing a component somewhere. And you perform these tests one at a time because you're more focused on just building the habit than on doing anything else.

REMEMBER

As you learn from these smaller tests, what you should be looking for is how the insights gained can impact other aspects of the site, app, or product. This way, when you scale up your tests, you have some data to show for why a bigger test may be more impactful.

TIP

When you first start testing, see whether you can launch just one test a week. You may find that even *that* is hard to do initially, because either communication gaps or accountability gaps occur. Fix what needs to be fixed by creating better documentation and setting better expectations, and try to reach that goal of one test per week. As you do, pay more attention to what you're learning from the weekly test, which could be anything from whether you set up the measurement for the test correctly (and if you didn't, rerun it with analytics set up correctly) to whatever small insights you gleaned from the test. As you learn, that should give you ideas for similar follow-on tests.

After you reach the goal of a single test a week for a couple of weeks in a row, add another test to the mix. If you can't get a second test launched, analyze why that happened and put in place a corrective measure to ensure that it doesn't happen again. If the reason you can't launch two tests is that you need more resources or people (like a designer or an engineer), here's where you need to start to make the (well-documented) case for why you need those resources to whoever has the power to provide them. (I talk a little more about this topic in the next section, because it can be a potential roadblock for your team.)

REMEMBER

Your goal is to do whatever it takes to reach the mark of two tests a week on an ongoing basis. If that means buying lunch every day for a couple of weeks, do it. All this is in the service of building the foundation for your culture of growth and learning.

This process only becomes more difficult as you try to reach three tests a week. By that time, you'll have long run out of "easy" tests to try, but you'll also have more data and more impact to share. You can start to make the case of how to extrapolate from the impact of those tests. You'll also have data-based justification for more resources, whether those are shared more formally now or are dedicated, whatever the case may be. What helps a lot here is having had the CEO buy in to the growth program so that they can use their influence to foster a culture of growth.

Making Your CEO the Growth Advocate

It's not an understatement to say that if your growth team is going to gain acceptance and succeed at what it does, it's because your team excels at sharing the insights it gains with the rest of the company. The trick to getting everyone in the company excited about this lies in making sure the CEO is excited about the growth team's work.

A well-functioning leadership team is essential to establishing your company culture and influencing organizational behavior. When the executive team, and especially the CEO, demonstrates excitement about the growth team's work, that sends a message about the importance of the team's work. And although the CEO's impact on the broader organization's excitement may be obvious, a couple of other dynamics are at play that make their involvement critical.

First and foremost, the growth team will be perceived as getting to have all the fun. After all, this is a team whose purpose is to push boundaries; they're not constrained by norms or what has happened before. Few other groups will have this level of (supposed) freedom. I say *supposed* because, if you've learned anything at all about growth hacking, it's that growth is a deliberate process. The impression that you get to do whatever the heck you want to do as a growth hacker is just that — an impression — and a rather dangerous one, at that. You need to nip that attitude in the bud by effectively communicating the serious nature of what your team is up to and why it matters to everyone. Without effective communication, pushback from teams who might be impacted by the growth team's work is inevitable, leading to unnecessary conflict. Who better than the CEO to get not only everyone's attention but also their buy-in?

The other issue is that someone is always ultimately responsible for the site or app that will be the object of all this testing. Any product will have a product team, engineers, and designers assigned to it. There will also be established processes around the development of any product. So your team will impact an established structure without really being the ultimate owner of whatever the team has been tasked with helping grow. Yes, you can have all the meetings you want in order to align your teams, but without an executive push to make it happen — no matter how well-oiled your culture — it will be difficult for such a working arrangement to stick.

REMEMBER

The CEO doesn't operate in a vacuum. The executive team is like a mini organization within the company that helps the CEO get work done. So, getting your CEO on board inevitably means getting your executive team on board with adopting this growth mentality.

There is no greater example of the embrace of a growth process than Jeff Bezos. He has attributed the success of Amazon to be a function of how many experiments employees carry out every day, every week, and every year. He clearly gets the fact that, even if the team has had ten failures in a row, that process has allowed them to come up with ideas, construct hypotheses, run tests, and fail fast, which means that the team is building momentum toward finding that inevitable big win.

THE MOST IMPORTANT MEETING YOU'LL EVER HAVE

After you have the CEO on board — especially when you've never had a growth program at the company before — have that person schedule a meeting with the rest of the executives. It can be set up for two hours to allow enough time to discuss the program, but prepare the team for the possibility that the meeting could last longer.

In this meeting, the executive team is brought into the fold. The why, what, and how is laid out for everyone to understand. This may even be the first time that the concept of the North Star Metric is brought up, which can lead to a vigorous debate about what this metric entails. The basic growth process, growth models, and so on are all explained in this meeting. After everyone begins to understand the cross-functional nature of the growth team, concerns may be raised about how things will work and how ownership may be impacted. All these topics are important discussions to have during this meeting. At the end of this meeting, everyone on the executive team should have committed to embracing the growth process and being a champion of it in their functional areas.

In fact, Bezos has gone as far as to say that one of the most distinctive aspects of Amazon is that it's the best place in the world to fail. He realizes that, if you want to come up with something new and innovative, you have to test — and that most of those tests will fail. The problem is that most company leaders aren't brave enough to endure all the failure needed to get to that point. And this license to be brave enough to fail repeatedly in the service of the customer really is the permission the CEO is giving everyone by cheerleading the growth initiative. This is how the executive team understands that testing is a worthy investment and that failure isn't to be feared.

Even with CEO buy-in, you may hit a couple of obstacles on your path to trying to build the right culture, with resources — or the lack thereof — as the first issue you'll run into (and fast). When you start with small tests, you mostly get small results. So, whenever you want to move on to more impactful tests and you need more resources, the first question you're asked is whether these resources are in fact justified. Pair that question with the reality that every company has finite resources, and it should come as no surprise that when it comes to choosing between testing and the sprint to release the next product, the sprint receives top priority.

This is where your choice for growth leader (hopefully) pays off. This is the person who can persuade others to give up some of their resources for "just a small thing." They're extremely scrappy about making it as easy as possible for the person in charge to sign off on whatever resource the tests need. If this means making promises of greater glory and recognition for being a risk-taker at some point down the road, they'll paint that picture most convincingly. Whoever is leading growth knows that getting these tests out the door is critical to building the right culture.

REMEMBER

The success rate of tests is low — very low. It's safe to say that leading with the statement "Yes, 80 to 90 percent of my tests fail" isn't a winning pitch. Even saying that you learn, of course, from every test doesn't help much because folks equate that statement with your wasting time and resources. So you need to perform a whole 'nother level of convincing, to prove that

>> The one or two tests that work are worth the effort.

>> The failed tests are worth even more effort.

>> Together, these are building blocks to a bigger result.

REMEMBER

The willingness to "beg, borrow, or steal" plays a huge part in your early success in laying the right foundation for a growth culture.

Sharing Is Better than Hoarding

The fact of the matter is, though the executive team is signaling buy-in and the growth team is dealing with the nitty-gritty of growth every week, the rest of the company is far removed from all this hullabaloo — they have their own daily work duties. So, they too must be brought into the fold and made to understand why the growth team exists and why everybody else should care about their work. This initial stage is all about setting expectations and providing education.

This process may end up requiring more than one meeting, but no matter how you schedule it, everyone in the company *must* attend so that they get to ask any questions they might have. In the end, everyone needs to understand the answers to basic questions, such as these:

>> What is our company's North Star Metric, why is it important, and why does it make sense for us?

>> What is our company's growth model, and how does the growth team use that information to focus their efforts?

>> Why was a certain objective chosen?

>> What does the testing process look like?

You're playing the part of the testing evangelist here and your goal is to communicate all of this in a way that generates excitement and enthusiasm for the program. To motivate your company effectively, you'll have to do more than just present these key points. You'll have to entertain your audience, do a fair amount of storytelling around the insights and the wins the program has already generated, and ask them to imagine the possibilities when everyone plays their part in the program.

Of course, the most important understanding that everyone needs to walk away with is why failure is a huge part of the process.

TIP

Irrespective of the size of your company when you begin a growth initiative, you have to supplement this initial education with more sessions, to ensure that everyone understands the key metrics being used. (The "lunch-and-learn" is a helpful format that you can conduct with internal and external experts.) And, even after these sessions conclude, you'll be well served if you create a knowledge base document that contains a glossary that defines all the metrics.

This education about the growth process also provides a chance to introduce simple workflows that make it easy for anyone to contribute testable ideas. (This can be as simple as a Google form.) By this time, if everyone has understood that growth is a cross-functional process, they should understand that they're all integral extensions of the growth team.

As you gather ideas from across the company, you can prioritize them appropriately. When you run a test that someone has submitted, you have an opportunity to go back and recognize the person who submitted the idea. Getting everyone in the company excited about the results of testing and making improvements to the product based on that input is the best way to bring everyone onboard with a culture of growth.

Weekly updates

After you've primed your organization to embrace whatever the growth team is doing, provide regular updates on what you're learning every week. Yes, this involves extra work on behalf of whoever on the team is assigned to share these updates, but it's not a task you can ignore. When sharing updates, you want to make it as easy as possible for everyone who isn't involved with the regular weekly meetings to understand what happened and what you learned.

Think seriously about every aspect of these weekly updates, such as when they're issued, their format, their content, and their dissemination. You have a lot riding on how successful you are in communicating the goals of the growth team to the rest of the organization.

Pick a specific day — say, the day you hold your growth meeting — as the day you send out this update to the rest of the company. Also pick a standard way of sharing it, whether it's an email, a dedicated channel of your internal communications platform, or a dedicated project-management tool. This creates an expectation and a habit among everyone that if it's, say, 3 o'clock on a Tuesday afternoon, it's time to check the weekly growth update.

One easy way to get people even more excited about results is to do send out a poll along with this update asking people to vote for what they think will be the winning variant for one of the tests in progress. Then, when you have results, share the names of the winners with the next update congratulating them for their awesome powers of guessing. From the pool of winners, randomly pick one person who gets a prize — some company swag, for example, or a $10 gift card that they can spend anywhere — and then share the winner's name as part of the update. This gamifies the involvement for the company, adds an element of fun, and keeps everyone eager for the next update.

The main thrust of this update is to share progress in terms of the current objectives and insights gained. To do this, ensure that you have a standard format that focuses on just a few items so that the update is easy to consume and understand. I like to think of this update in the same way as I would think about an update I'd give the CEO — short, sweet, and to the point.

However you choose to display the information, it should contain these items:

>> The current measurement of the NSM

>> The NSM trend (for at least the past four weeks)

>> Current objectives and how you're doing against them

>> Any three (or so) other key top-level metrics

>> The number of ideas added to the backlog last week as well as the top contributors

>> The number of experiments run last week

>> The number of experiments added to the knowledge base last week

>> The top insights gained from last week's experiments

>> The experiment failure (or success) rate to-date

The goal of sharing weekly updates is to share information that only the growth team may be considering. This format also ensures complete transparency within the company because it reports both the good news and the bad news. When numbers aren't moving in the right direction, these reports can help instill a sense of urgency within the company. But even when things aren't working well, it's important to frame everything in the context of what has been learned. This strategy helps maintain a positive impression when you have a lot of failed tests. When things are going well, though, that's cause to celebrate, and to pull together to get even more wins to keep the momentum going.

Monthly deep dives

Every month, invite everyone in the company to revisit those tests that provided the team with their deepest insights. Most of them will likely not remember individual tests from the weekly updates, so it's worth the effort to ask people, by a show of hands, which test won. Expect many of them to still pick the wrong answer. These "deep dives" will further help cement the growth team's impact and reinforce the fact that assumptions or opinions are often wrong, which is why testing is needed. As you repeat this exercise, you also communicate the core principles of growth, over and over, to the rest of the company.

TIP

During the monthly meeting, or even within your regularly scheduled meeting of all hands on deck, start with a customer success story. This would be something you'd have to plan for every time by talking to customers who are deriving value from your product and understanding what greater thing your product enables for them. Put one of those stories together as a 2 to 3 slide presentation or a 2- to 3-minute video that communicates how your product helps that customer. Not only does this start the meeting off on a great note, but it also serves to reinforce the value of the product and the importance of the growth program in increasing the value the product provides. By making the customer the hero of the story, it serves as a source of inspiration underscoring the fact that, when everyone participates with growth, the company enables even greater things.

You can also add an element of fun by presenting a Best Failed Test award to one person whose idea was tested. This sort of appreciation encourages others in the organization who haven't yet participated in the growth process to dip their toes into the world of testing, because they'll literally see failure being rewarded in the context of growth.

You can even consider installing a prominently displayed "failure board," updated occasionally with the names of tests and the people who submitted those tests (assuming that people are okay with this idea). This way, passersby gain ongoing, high-level exposure to others' ideas that have been tried. (It might even awaken a desire to get their own names on that board!)

Quarterly updates

As you continue testing and sending updates, people tend to forget about the tests — and certainly the failed tests that produced this result: "I never would have expected that." A quarterly "failure report" helps people remember. The name certainly has a ring to it, which is why it also garners attention. Other than calling out the biggest failed tests, it helps everyone recall what the team learned from these tests.

REMEMBER

Reading the updates doesn't have to be a boring task, by any stretch of the imagination. Make them fun and lively because reading them plays a part in reinforcing a culture of learning and in keeping everyone interested in the testing process.

The not-so-hidden agenda behind sharing insights with the rest of the company weekly, monthly, and quarterly is to solicit more ideas. Every time employees are exposed to a test and the resulting insights gained, someone, somewhere, in the company will circle around and ask whether you've tried the test in a different way or analyzed it for a certain data point. This is a good circumstance, because feedback from people not immersed in the day-to-day detail of growth sometimes opens your eyes to problems directly in front of you that you missed.

The other major goal of sharing any insights gained company-wide is to instill a culture of testing, learning, and growth. Such a culture is one where everyone is ready to

>> Test everything, big and small

>> Run well-planned tests with clear results that drive action

>> Fail often and fast and learn from those failures

>> Pay attention to the results of qualitative and quantitative data

>> Keep testing and learning every day, every week, and every year

Figure 11-1 gives a graphical view of these main ideas.

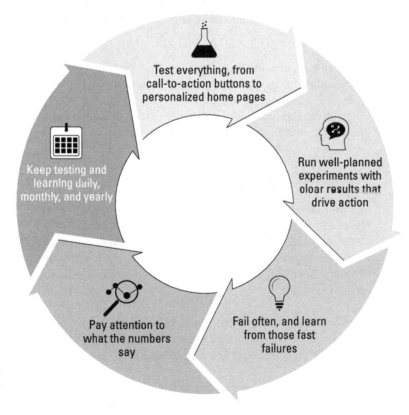

FIGURE 11-1:
Culture of growth
and learning.

Fostering a culture of growth is an ongoing process that takes a lot of work. By design, it makes some people in the company uncomfortable, and it certainly forces people out of their comfort zones. And, of course, you'll fail. A lot. But if you want to achieve cross-functional collaboration around growth, happier customers, and more value delivered to them, you have no choice but to go down this path. Building this culture takes time, but it's the way to unlock growth that you may not be able to access otherwise.

If you succeed in instilling a culture of growth, you'll inadvertently hit on the curse of winning. If everyone now wants to get involved with testing but the knowledge of what makes a great test varies, you might have people running meaningless tests and contributing to waste. That may entail your having to invest in more formal training (put together by the growth team itself based on their own practices) to ensure that everyone has a base level of understanding key concepts before they can get involved in any testing program.

The other problem you might face is that, with different teams running tests, you could have tests unintentionally overlapping one other, contaminating the results. To avoid that situation, you may have to create both approval and scheduling processes that ensure this doesn't happen, even if it means that teams have to move a little slower than normal.

Another issue can arise when leaders are just a tad too enthusiastic. It may sound like a good idea to challenge your team to run a hundred tests in a quarter, but that can lead to scattershot "test blasts" that don't reveal (or help) anything. Make sure that tests are well-run, in an orderly succession, with controls for all variables that may be involved.

4

The Part of Tens

Chapter **12**

Ten Key Benefits of the Growth Hacking Methodology

n this chapter, I summarize ten important benefits that the growth hacking methodology provides to organizations and products. Keep in mind that, in order to take full advantage of the growth hacking process, you need to have buy-in at the highest levels of the organization and establish trust with other teams so that you can focus everyone's efforts on whatever delivers the greatest value to your customers.

A Focus on Process versus Tactics

If you take away only one lesson from this book, I hope that it's this: Growth hacking is a process. Sustainable growth can come only from growing value for your customers on an ongoing basis. The growth process helps you understand where the strategic focus of your team's growth efforts should be, which in turn produces ideas for you to test that lead to specific tactical decisions for your team to act on.

Tactics, on their own and without the benefit of a strategy, are like a rudderless boat with no direction. You may find yourself running a lot of tests and maybe even generating a lot of wins, but without this focus, you'll disperse your learning potential, which minimizes the impact you can have on your North Star Metric — leaving you with no clear way to move forward.

Here are two syndromes to be wary of when it comes to tactics:

» **Copycat syndrome:** The tactics you may have read about that worked spectacularly for others may not work as well (or at all) for you. Everyone's products are different, the audiences are different, and the overall context is different. Too many variables are at play to take at face value all those online articles titled "X Ways We Increased Y by Z Percent." It's more important to understand *why* a company acted the way it did — its process, in other words — than what it did. Without that background understanding, you might take the wrong lessons from such content.

» **Shareholder value syndrome:** Worse are the tactics that are detrimental to the overall customer experience and deliver little to no value to them. These may be great at demonstrating how someone took advantage of a loophole in a system or exploited certain human biases, but if those tactics were more to benefit the business than the customers, you have to ask what the long-term impact of those tactics might be on the overall brand and perception of the company. When in doubt, err on the side of the customer's gaining more from an interaction.

It's fair to say that, in the absence of a better understanding of what growth hacking is about, people can easily (and incorrectly) associate these spammy tactics and tricks with growth hacking as such and deride the overall practice.

Cross-Functional Collaboration

The greatest benefit of implementing a growth process is its ability to break down *silos* — those artificial "walls" between different groups within the company. A North Star Metric gives everyone a single point of focus. The ability to test needs resources from across the organization, and getting them, requires key stakeholders (including the CEO) to buy into the process. Make no mistake: This is hard to do — and increasingly harder the more the culture of the organization is already set.

TIP

Having representation from key stakeholders in product, engineering, sales, creative, and analytics teams in the weekly growth meeting allows for a more holistic reality check for ideas that are proposed for testing.

A well-implemented growth process also democratizes where ideas come from and allows you to take advantage of insights from across the organization that you might otherwise not have been able to access.

Organizational Alignment

A natural consequence of cross-functional collaboration is alignment across the company. A North Star Metric (NSM) allows everyone, irrespective of team status, to ask, "How is what I'm doing today helping move the needle on our NSM?" This is a powerful question for individuals to pose to themselves as well as managers to pose to their direct reports during meetings. If someone cannot articulate how their work will impact the NSM, it's time to reprioritize tasks so that the person has a better response the next time this question is asked.

When an entire company is focused on growing the NSM, you have a company that is rowing the proverbial boat in sync.

Data-Informed Decision-Making

The biggest trap that many companies fall into is using feelings, opinions, and hearsay to inform major business decisions. The problem with such approaches goes beyond not being objective. Generally, only the people at the top of the organizational food chains can get away with statements along the lines of, "I think we should do this or that." This fuels the wrong culture — one that's more about satisfying egos or doing as you're told because raising your hand, so to speak, will only cause more trouble.

Data takes all this conjecture out of the picture and rewards those hypotheses that are proven true. You're telling everyone that no one gets to hijack growth and that everyone has a part to play. By injecting data into the company's DNA, you create transparency into what's working and what's not. This allows anyone in the company to ask clarifying questions of the growth team or to propose new ideas.

Improved Customer Focus

The beauty of the NSM is that it's entirely customer focused. If you grow the value that you deliver to the customer, by definition you raise the odds of your own success. By having a number that everyone cares about be all about the customer, you're better able to mitigate any bickering about individual team metrics and priorities because now the customer-focused metric is the most important one.

This isn't to say that the numbers for which teams are held accountable aren't important. If anything, they should all roll up to the NSM. But by having a common, customer-focused number that everyone cares about that supersedes every other number, you actively convey the message that everyone is in charge of delivering and growing customer value. This is no longer the job of only the onboarding, customer success, or retention team. It's *everyone's* job.

A Better Understanding of Your Customers

If growth hacking is all about growing the value you deliver to the customer, it behooves you to understand your customers' motivations so that you can help them achieve their goals. This is not to say that this is a one-time exercise. To help customers continue to derive value from your product, you have to understand at what frequency they need to use your product and where your product fits into the scheme of their lives. You'll also find out why people stop using your product to learn. If you cannot determine who out there your product isn't a fit for or what was lacking from your end that caused them to give up your product, even if they found value from it, you've lost a growth opportunity.

Beyond that, though you may start off serving a specific kind of customer, over time you will encounter many different types of people, with their own reasons for using your product. You'll (have to) learn how to serve all these people in the way they want to be served, if they're going to keep using your product over the long term. Again, the beauty of the NSM is that it's explicit about quantifying value delivered so that, as you gain a better understanding of your customers, the NSM will lead you down paths to serve them better.

Improved Customer Experience

If understanding your customers better is one side of the coin, the other side is all about delivering a better and more relevant experience for them. Your hard work in decoding their needs will produce a natural affinity for your product because few other products will have taken as much trouble to focus on their goals.

Having the mentality "How else can we add value for you?" — where you're constantly in touch with your customers — reveals new avenues to serve them. Here, too, you'll find categories of customers who have similar needs that you can address in unique ways. As you travel down this path, you'll gain further insights that allow you to slice your customer segments into smaller and smaller pieces. The logical end point will appear like a hyperpersonalized experience for each customer. It's a difficult path to travel, for sure, but if you use personalized experiences as a simple way to visualize how far you need to go to serve each and every customer, it has a natural impact on the kinds of activities you choose to engage in to deliver that value.

A State of Constant Curiosity

To uncover your customers' needs, you have to be in constant detective mode. The mystery of how to deliver value, as I just mentioned, has many layers. You can't sit there happy with having found only a single insight. If you do, you'll inevitably see the impact on your growth metrics — they'll move in the wrong direction.

Finding insights that drive growth, however, is addicting. Whether that needle moves slowly or quickly, you'll be on the hunt for that next key insight. This need infects everyone on the growth team. So, whether its learning directly from customers or from external inspiration, if you're looking to grow value, you'll also be looking for a whole series of different ways to grow that value, perhaps in ways you (or your customers) never expected and that are in keeping with the ethos of growth hacking.

Better Product-Development Processes

I always strongly recommend that the product team be represented in growth meetings. Product managers, generally speaking, oversee the product features and how they're brought to life. Their presence is vital to ensure that tests that have produced winners are incorporated into the product development cycle with as little disruption to existing plans as possible but also with an eye toward expediency. The best product managers will either have a dedicated stream of work for incorporating winning tests into the process or, if this isn't possible, build the need to do so into their existing plans. Having the ability to incorporate insights gained from ongoing testing into the planned product development process can only help amplify the impact of the product to your customers.

Greater Control because of Product-First Growth

Channels are changing all the time. If your growth is highly dependent on external channels, you need to be careful: You have zero control over when these channels will change and whether such changes will negatively impact your growth. Because growth hacking focuses on the entire customer journey, the product itself plays a greater part in growth.

Yes, you have to scale acquisition, but retention is the name of the game after you have someone's attention. After someone has decided to check out your product, *you* are in charge. Every aspect of their experience, big and small, is in your hands, which means that you can test and learn far more effectively about what a great first experience looks like and what it will take to

>> Inspire people to come back to experience that core value of your product

>> Monetize the value your product delivers

>> Make it easy for your customers to spread the word about you

IN THIS CHAPTER

» Recognizing that cheerleading is the key

» Staying focused

» Prioritizing testing

» Taking chances

» Striking out on your own

» Focusing on insights gained, not tasks achieved

» Factoring in the opportunity costs of testing

» Running good tests (not bad ones)

» Sticking to a schedule

» Revisiting (and rethinking) past successes

Chapter **13**

Ten Things to Watch Out For

G rowth teams can make common but serious mistakes when implementing the growth process. This chapter provides an overview of some of the more typical problems and looks at ways for you to work around them.

As you'll see, many of these pitfalls are related to cultural issues and usually result from not following the established process itself. Let the data and your empathy for the customer guide you and you'll mitigate most of the problems that afflict growth teams who are just starting out.

Ignoring the Need to Constantly Evangelize Progress and Learning

To me, an inability to sing from the rooftops the praises of the growth process is probably the biggest stumbling block when it comes to creating a company-wide culture of growth. Especially as you're getting your growth program off the ground, you have to be able to evangelize experimentation and share those quick wins in high-decibel fashion. When the business isn't used to operating this way, seeing data for the first time can create a sense of empowerment throughout the organization.

REMEMBER

Be consistent with what, how, and where you communicate progress when it comes to growth. Whether it's an internal wiki, an internal communication platform channel, email, company-wide meetings, lunch-and-learns, or any other venue, posting summaries of tests and the insights the team gleaned leads to greater understanding and adoption of the growth mentality. Ultimately, your goal is to build company-wide excitement for the program in order to break down silos and gather input from every corner of the company on ideas that hold growth potential.

Not Sticking to the Growth Meeting Agenda

From personal experience, I can tell you that the one hour you set aside for the weekly growth meeting goes by *fast.* Having an agenda and sticking to it is critical for working your way through communicating key metrics, sharing the insights gained from the past week, and then deciding on tests to prioritize in the next testing cycle. You should expect that additional questions may emerge when discussing what happened last week, but you absolutely cannot afford to let the agenda be derailed by anyone, especially if they're someone higher up in the organization.

REMEMBER

For good reason, the agenda of the growth meeting has fixed time slots for discussing specific aspects of growth. If the discussion extends beyond the allotted time, end the meeting with a commitment to pick it up again later, and communicate a summary with the rest of the team. (For more on running a growth meeting, see Chapter 10.)

The other common trap is for the growth meeting to become a brainstorming session. Avoid this at all costs. All brainstorming should happen *between* growth meetings. Within the meeting, you simply discuss ideas that have already been prioritized from the backlog before the meeting. If you don't impose some discipline here, you won't be able to establish the rhythm of a growth process.

Testing Things That Don't Need to Be Tested (Right Now)

When you first start testing and you're looking for quick wins, it's okay to not necessarily be informed by your growth model. But as you gain a bit of confidence, you can't afford to be scattershot about it. I've fallen into this trap as well, where we met the goal of conducting three or more tests per week but barely moved the needle on our NSM, which was incredibly frustrating.

I understand the lure of testing in areas you're comfortable with, yet you cannot allow yourself to do only the simple things or the ones you like doing. Growth is about doing more of what works. Finding out what works is a matter of investigating your growth model and setting objectives around the highest leverage opportunities (or problems). (For more on setting objectives, see Chapter 7.)

Not Taking Big Enough Swings

Recognizing a big swing when it comes to tests isn't obvious when you start. In fact, almost everything looks like a big change the first time it's made, because something like that has never been done. It's important, however, for the team to undertake the process of making swings that aren't big enough and to realize the small impact, if any, on your NSM. That's when the light bulb will go off — the team will realize that what they *thought* was a big deal really wasn't. This will trigger discussions on what it truly means to be big.

Undertaking this process of taking swings and realizing you can go bigger is necessary for the team to build the courage to take bigger swings and also realize that they have permission to do so.

REMEMBER

This is not to say that small wins don't matter; of course they do. But the bigger wins come when you do something so radically different that the reaction to it *has* to be big. If that reaction happens to be a positive one, you'll see it reflected in your NSM. Then take all the small swings you want, to incrementally make that big positive result as big as you can. Just be aware that small tests give you small results. If you want big results, conduct bigger, bolder tests. It's as simple (and as hard) as that.

Blindly Copying What Others Have Done

You'll find no dearth of articles espousing awesome results from tests. It's these types of posts that have led people to think that growth hacking is all about tactics. This isn't to say that you shouldn't be inspired by others. Of course you should. External sources of inspiration are a powerful source of ideas.

It's important to understand *why* a test worked rather than get caught up in the tactic that resulted in spectacular results. This is why, if you were to blindly implement a referral program, like the Dropbox example, or create a contest offering an iPad as a prize, it likely wouldn't produce the same breakout results as in others.

REMEMBER

Understanding your own users' motivations and knowing what they value should guide your strategies more than what has worked for famous companies or for competitors.

Measuring What You Did versus What You Learned

It's easy to get caught up in running tests and increasing conversion rates. (I've fallen into this common trap, too.) If you didn't add value for your customers, however, all that just isn't very meaningful — and therein lies the difference between what you did (your *outputs*) versus what you learned about helping your customers achieve their goals (your *outcomes*).

You should understand that, ultimately, customers are interested only in outcomes — the benefit they receive from your product. This can happen only if you understand their needs, priorities, motivations, and challenges. What you did, on the other hand (running tests or optimizing your product, for example) is just an output of the growth process. Measuring what you learned about delivering value is ultimately what creates the biggest difference in your customers' lives, so make sure you're measuring the right things.

Not Understanding the Opportunity Costs of Testing

Failing to understand the opportunity costs of testing goes hand in hand with running tests that don't need to be run right now. Every test has an opportunity cost associated with it, and you need to calculate how much more value a test provides versus doing more research.

Now, if you can conduct a quick test all by yourself and it doesn't interfere with another test, just do it, because there's no downside here. But if you're doing something more involved or what you're doing deals with an integral part of the product, any changes here could have a noticeable negative impact. In this case, check to see whether you have enough data to justify a test, and reduce the amount of uncertainty associated with that test.

The other opportunity cost is related to not being able to identify tests that are actually winners. Sample size and test duration both impact your ability to call a true winner, but the longer any given test runs, you also potentially risk losing out on bigger gains from other, more impactful tests. Think about the size of the insight you're testing for before determining how much resources and time you allocate to any given test.

TIP

Committing to a process where you run big, bold tests to discover big changes in response, followed by the smaller tests to optimize that response, helps mitigate some of that opportunity cost.

Having Lots of Tests That Yield Inconclusive Results

First, you can expect tests now and then to yield inconclusive results. (See Chapter 9 for more on that topic.) It's bound to happen. What should *not* happen is that it becomes normal to see inconclusive results for tests. This situation occurs for one of these reasons:

>> You lacked a good hypothesis to begin with.

>> The experiment itself wasn't designed well.

>> You didn't set up how to measure the test correctly.

>> The analysis itself was incomplete.

   This last reason is the most difficult to correct for, because the others are related more to process issues, which you should analyze and correct the first time you encounter them.

The bigger problem that emerges is the fact that, if you have inconclusive results, you don't learn anything. A test you didn't learn from is effectively wasted, which adds to the opportunity cost of testing. Continually encountering these dead ends can become quite demoralizing. They start to instill apathy regarding testing, in the sense that everyone starts to expect that conducting a certain number of tests will be wasted effort, no matter what. This can have a negative impact on the effort that people invest in tests, and the result can be extremely insidious, leading to a negative feedback loop of less interest and effort, leading to bad tests with inconclusive results, leading to *even less* enthusiasm for the next round of tests.

Not Analyzing Your Tests in a Timely Fashion

This one hurts. Running a lot of tests is one thing, and you can get a lot of the process right by creating the right objectives and generating a lot of ideas to test. But running tests and leaving them unanalyzed is the kiss of death to a growth program. After all, growth involves learning more about what works. How else will you do more of it?

I've experienced this problem firsthand, where I was responsible for analyzing acquisition tests related to selling more tickets for an event. Because I took longer to analyze these tests, we didn't learn about some opportunities we could have capitalized on, and that inevitably led to selling fewer tickets than usual. You can be sure I've never let it happen again. As I mention in the earlier section "Not Understanding the Opportunity Costs of Testing," not capitalizing on a win is also costly.

On the topic of acquisition, because we have no control over how channels will change, it's even more important to stay on top of such tests. You may find that, although an initial test gave you positive results, if you waited too long to learn about it and the channel evolved in a way that's unfriendly to that specific tactic, future tests won't work. So it's doubly important to analyze your acquisition tests quickly, to get an early sign that things might be changing so you can adapt in a timely manner.

Not Checking on Whether the Gains Still Hold

When you're in the rhythm of testing, and launching tests weekly, it's easy to forget about tests you've already analyzed. They're in the knowledge base, but out of sight and out of mind.

The problem is that no winning test provides infinite gains — not to mention the fact that most tests have small gains. You should have a process to go back and analyze how well the gains of any winning test have held over time and whether the gains show signs of decreasing (or have already decreased). You can use that information as a trigger to perform a new test around the area that provided the gain.

Without this information, you'll feel like you're running in place or, even worse, like your momentum slows because the efficiency of earlier tests that you were counting on as stepping stones is no longer available to you.

To start, it may be useful to review the winning tests every couple of months to see how well they're performing and then adjust from there.

Chapter **14**

Ten (+Twelve!) Key Resources to Continue Your Education

Many organizations, websites, podcasts, blogs, communities, and companies exist to provide information about and support for growth hacking (even if they don't explicitly say so). To help you get started, I've compiled a list of key resources (in no particular order) that I've used and continue to refer to and that you, too, can use to support your journey with growth hacking.

These have intentionally been picked for their broad applicability across the customer journey and to the growth process in general, rather than a specific part of the journey.

GrowthHackers.com

http://growthhackers.com

The GrowthHackers site probably contains the largest curated database of the highest-quality growth content around. Discussions around this content, questions about all aspects of growth hacking, and Ask Me Anything (AMA) sessions with subject matter experts ensure that you'll have ample growth content for continual learning.

CXL Blog

https://cxl.com/blog

CXL (formerly known as ConversionXL) has been churning out high-quality, in-depth marketing, analytics, and optimization content by offering a combination of in-house and guest posts by subject matter experts. The site's stated goal is to make the knowledge and insights possessed by the best experts in their field accessible to anyone who's motivated enough to take advantage of them.

Optimizely Blog

https://blog.optimizely.com

The Optimizely blog, operated by the company that owns the popular A/B testing tool, mostly features its own team of optimization experts, who share their best advice on A/B testing and experience optimization. The site also tends to dig deeper into the process than most growth-oriented blogs.

Conversion Sciences Blog

https://conversionsciences.com/conversion-optimization-blog

The Conversion Optimization blog aims to teach digital marketers how to embrace data and science in their work. The blog is organized into three main levels of mastery: conversion rate optimization (CRO) 101 for beginners, conversion rate optimization (CRO) 102 for intermediate, and conversion rate optimization (CRO) 103 for advanced, so you choose your level and start learning.

Reforge Blog

www.reforge.com/blog

Reforge, led by Brian Balfour and Andrew Chen, has created lots of must-read content that takes a more holistic view of growth than most other sites. Almost all the content, which is a combination of posts by the Reforge team and guest contributors, is focused on strategy and process.

Brian Balfour's Blog

https://brianbalfour.com

Brian Balfour also maintains his own site, where he's been producing in-depth essays for years on building a machine of sustainable growth. He appears to have stopped posting on this site in favor of the Reforge blog starting in 2019, but the content that's still on his blog is evergreen and worth revisiting over and over again.

Andrew Chen's Blog

https://andrewchen.co

Andrew Chen's blog features long-form essays on start-ups, growth, metrics, and network effects. An investor at Andreessen Horowitz — where he focuses on consumer products, marketplaces, and bottoms-up SaaS — he shares from these experiences and more.

Intercom Blog

www.intercom.com/blog

The Inside Intercom team members share thoughts, tips, and lessons learned from their years of product building and developing sales, marketing, and customer support. The site doesn't position itself as a growth resource, but given that it tackles various aspects of building great products, it truly is one and provides valuable perspectives on how to deliver value.

Occam's Razor Blog

www.kaushik.net/avinash

Possibly one of the best blogs on analytics for its ability to make the topic easy for everyone to understand, Avinash Kaushik's site provides practical takes on how to unlock the power of research and analytics to create a data-driven culture.

Analytics Demystified Blog

https://analyticsdemystified.com/blog

Another helpful resource for all analytics topics, from setup to measurement and reporting, the Analytics Demystified blog stays on top of the latest developments with analytics tools and presents content on everything from strategy and imple-mentation to testing and reporting.

MeasuringU Blog

https://measuringu.com/blogs

This blog, from the quantitative research firm MeasuringU, specifically centers around usability, customer experience, and statistics.

Online Behavior Blog

https://online-behavior.com

This blog is a useful knowledge source when it comes to understanding how online customers behave. The site understands and espouses a broad range of techniques and strategies to help optimize websites and provides content on targeting and segmentation, site testing and usability, as well as analytics and optimization.

Casey Winters' Blog

https://caseyaccidental.com

Casey Winters has been an early (if not the first) marketer at many high-profile start-ups. His experiences in scaling multiple start-ups to large technology companies as an employee and an advisor inform his wide perspective on growth that few other people can match.

Kieran Flanagan's Blog

www.kieranflanagan.io/blog

Kieran, the VP of marketing at HubSpot, has a proven track record in helping SaaS businesses — from start-ups to enterprise-level — grow their traffic, users, and revenue. His blog posts about founders or senior executives at different companies investigate which unique aspects of growth they might be handling effectively. In his podcast (which he cohosts), he conducts weekly interviews with subject matter experts to understand strategies that have helped the best companies in the world grow.

Growth Engineering Blog

www.growthengblog.com

The blog of Jeff Chang, who leads growth teams at Pinterest as a technical lead, focuses on conversions, user engagement and retention, mobile acquisition, A/B testing, data analysis, and other topics on growth based on his firsthand experience.

Widerfunnel Blog

www.widerfunnel.com/blog

The Widerfunnel digital marketing agency has championed experimentation from the start. Its content covers everything from process to culture to tactics and trends sweeping through the industry. The posts are written by a combination of the site's internal team and experts who've had firsthand experience in driving the experimentation methodology across industries.

forEntrepeneurs Blog

www.forentrepreneurs.com/

forEntrepreneurs is a blog by David Skok, a venture capitalist at Matrix Partners. The blog is an in-depth resource that offers advice on the key issues founders and their teams face in getting started, getting funded, and building a successful company. This blog has some of the best resources on go-to-market strategies and metrics. Even though the focus is on SaaS products, the content here applies to most products.

Mobile Growth Stack Blog

https://mobilegrowthstack.com/

Mobile Growth Stack is a publication by Phiture, a leading mobile growth consultancy. Phiture's co-founder, Andy Carvell, used to be the mobile growth lead at Soundcloud. This is probably the most useful resource I've found for content on how to develop and evolve a strategy for growing the user base of a mobile product.

Dan Wolchonok's Blog

www.danwolch.com/

Dan Wolchonok works with Brian Balfour and is the head of product at Reforge. He admittedly hasn't write much and much to my dismay writes even less nowadays. But what he has written on the topics of retention and analytics is content you will not find anywhere else. He's a highly technical growth professional and some of his content around data analysis is very advanced.

Christoph Janz's Blog

http://christophjanz.blogspot.com/

Christoph Janz is a partner at Point Nine Capital. He shares his thoughts on startups, SaaS, and early-stage investing here. He doesn't write as frequently as he used to on growth related topics either but, like Dan Wolchonok, his content on retention, business models, and strategy is very unique, evergreen, and explained very simply.

The Amplitude Blog

https://amplitude.com/blog

Amplitude, a behavioral analytics software company, shares perspectives and best practices on product management, building products, user retention, growth, engagement, and more on its blog. This blog is often my first stop when looking for answers, especially when I'm looking for deeper insights on retention.

The Breakout Growth Podcast

www.seanellis.me/the-breakout-growth-podcast.html

In this podcast, Sean Ellis interviews CEOs and product, growth, and marketing leaders from the world's fastest-growing companies to strike at the heart of what truly drives their breakout growth. This way, you can apply their lessons to take your growth to the next level. Discussions cover everything from the role of mission and product/market fit in driving growth to team structure and leadership style to specific tests and tactics used to accelerate growth.

Glossary

A/B testing Creating two versions of a product, usually by changing one element at a time, testing both, and comparing the results to see which one performed best.

AARRR An acronym representing a simplified customer journey developed by Dave McClure of 500 Startups. The acronym stands for Acquisition, Activation, Retention, Revenue, and Referral.

acquisition All the different ways people find out about your product.

activation The sequence of events that leads to someone understanding the value of your product to them. Your goal is to get people to experience this at the earliest, right time to raise the odds of their continuing to use your product.

aha moment The moment the "light bulb" goes off in someone's mind that your product satisfies their needs.

backlog The area where growth ideas are stored that are waiting to be prioritized and tested. This area can be as simple as a spreadsheet or a specific tool to help organize ideas. The ideas in the backlog are prioritized using different methodologies and then put into the testing workflow when the time is right.

churn rate The number of customers you lose over a given period, or when customers stop using your product. Churn is the opposite of customer retention.

cohort analysis A way of grouping users by specific criteria, such as the date they signed up or the acquisition channel they came from, and examining how these groups behave, in order to be able to extract insights from their product experience.

conversion rate The measure of the number of people who complete a specific action or the number of times a specific action is completed after someone has the opportunity to perform that specific action, after generating an impression. For example, the number of users who provide an email address after visiting your website.

conversion rate optimization A systematic process of increasing the percentage of visitors who take a desired action with your product. It involves understanding what they do and don't do within your product to gain insights into how you can remove roadblocks to their using your product or make using your product more efficient for themselves.

experiment A process in which you apply the scientific method to testing an idea and validating (or invalidating) a hypothesis; also called a *test*.

growth hacker A person dedicated to increasing the value that a product delivers to customers by understanding their motivations and using a combination of creativity and data to identify the best ways to provide that value.

growth hacking A cross-functional process that is based on testing and learning about opportunities for breakout growth that are sustainable. The impact of growth hacking is measured by a number called the North Star Metric (see the later definition).

hacking The *hacking* in growth hacking refers to the innovative, inventive, and creative ways someone uses to find avenues that can lead to increases in the growth rate of the product.

Minimum Viable Product (MVP) An early version of the product (that may not even look like the final product) that can be released and tested with a small set of users to learn about the value the product provides (or not). You iterate on your MVP to validate whether you have product market fit (see the later definition).

North Star Metric (NSM) The one number that quantifies the value your product delivers to your customers or users. Every product is different because the value it provides is different and hence the NSM will be unique for every business.

objective The current focus area of the growth process, where most of the tests will be run. Objectives keep changing as you look at the results of your testing.

One Metric That Matters (OMTM) The one number that quantifies an objective. Just as objectives keep changing, the OMTM also changes, based on the focus area.

product-market fit The stage at which you have validated that your product meets a real need for a significant number of people. This is the minimum necessary condition to start growth hacking.

sprint A given period (normally, one or two weeks) when the growth team works to launch ideas to test.

T-shaped A way of describing the depth and breadth of skills a growth professional needs to acquire to be effective at their job, visualized in the shape of a *T*. The line on top represents the breadth of knowledge, and the vertical line represents the depth of knowledge.

vanity metrics Metrics that have no real value and cannot help you make critical business decisions, such as likes on a Facebook post.

Index

B

backlogs
  creating, 17
  of ideas
    adding, 118
    building, 14
Baker, Ed, 107
Balfour, Brian
  blog by, 211
  inventing T-shaped marketer, 28
  methodology for prioritizing channels by, 87
  as owner of Reforge Blog, 211
bandit and multivariate, 149–151
base knowledge layer
  basic HTML and CSS as part of, 30
  behavioral psychology as part of, 29
  branding as part of, 29
  design as part of, 29–30
  overview, 28
  positioning as part of, 29
  statistics fundamentals as part of, 30
  storytelling as part of, 29
  user experience design as part of, 29–30
Behavior, in Google Analytics, 66
behavioral analytics
  basics of, 70–71
  implementing
    with Amplitude, 73–75
    overview, 71–73
behavioral characteristics, of growth hackers, 33–38
behavioral psychology, 29
Bezos, Jeff, 184–185
blind to nonlinearity, 63
blogs, targeting
  as part of channel expertise layer, 32
  as way of to acquire users, 84
brainstorming, 203
branding, 29
breadth, 159
Breakout Growth podcast, 215
Brinker, Scott, 64

Brown, Morgan
  description of growth hacking by, 15–16
  on job title misconception, 22
  onboarding and activation, 91
Bush, Wes, 18
business. *See also* companies
  assessing growth of, 76
  growth audits and, 76–77
  product-led growth and, 18
  sustainability and, 11–12
business development, 84

C

calls to action (CTAs)
  defined, 123
  of other companies, 122
Campbell, Joseph, 79–80
Campbell, Patrick, 98
capitalizing
  on tests, 15
  on wins, 205
Carvell, Andy, 214
Cascading Style Sheets (CSS), 30
CEO (chief executive officer). *See also* growth leads
  fostering culture of growth in companies, 183
  growth teams and, 183–185
  as head of growth
    de facto, 172
    starting growth team, 43
Chang, Jeff, 213
changes
  systemizing, 162–163
  during testing, 182–183
channel expertise layer
  affiliate programs as part of, 32
  community building as part of, 33
  content marketing as part of, 32
  email marketing as part of, 32
  engineering as marketing as part of, 32
  existing platforms as part of, 32
  offline ads as part of, 32

empowering companies, 202

excessive amount of, 74

internal

  overview, 120

  user experience insights, 121

  user flow insights, 120

quantitative vs. qualitative, 125

sharing, 175

taking decisions based on

  benefits of, 197

  emotion vs., 132

data analyst, 41

data and analytics, 30

decisions

  based on data, making, 197

  organizational cultures influencing, 52–53

depth, 159

design, 29–30

Destination, in Google Analytics, 68

developing products, 199–200

display ads, 84

dominance, defined, 34

Duration, in Google Analytics, 68

E

ease

  in ICE score, 132

  in PIE framework, 135

efficiency, 160

effort, in RICE score, 137

Eisenberg, Bryan, 136

Ellis, Sean

  Ask Me Anything session with, 16–17

  on CEO and head of growth, 172

  equation for conversion rate optimization (CRO), 106–107

  growth meetings and, 166

  on high-tempo testing, 104

  ICE score and, 133

  inventing phrase, 10, 19

  on learning, 155

  optimizing growth meetings, 166

  podcast by, 215

  survey by, 12

Elman, Josh, 91

email marketing

  as part of channel expertise layer, 32

  as way of to acquire users, 84

engineering, as types of resource categories, 145

engineering as marketing

  as part of channel expertise layer, 32

  as way of to acquire users, 84

equations

  for conversion rate optimization (CRO), 106–107

  for growth, 112–114

  for RICE score, 137

Event, in Google Analytics, 68

existing platforms

  as part of channel expertise layer, 32

  as way of to acquire users, 84

expected results, in scientific method, 104

experience, for customers

  improving, 199

  misconception regarding, 19

exploring, business measurements, 76–77

exploring organizational culture, 48

external sources, 121–122

externally focused, 47

extraversion, defined, 34

F

Facebook, 107

factors, defined, 34

Flanagan, Kieran, 213

flexibility, 47

flow diagram, 120

focusing

  on customers, 198

  on objectives, 118–119

forEntrepeneurs website, 214

formality, defined, 34

I

ICE score, 133–134
ideas. *See also* testing
  backlog of, 14
  brainstorming, 203
  contributing, 171
  growth and, 195
  nominating, 170–171
  soliciting for, 189
  for testing, choosing
    external sources, 121–122
    internal data, 120–121
    overview, 119–122
  for testing, prioritizing, 131–141
inconclusive tests
  defined, 155
  excessive, 205–206
  learning from, 161–162
independent-led model, 44
individualist workstyle, 36–37
influence
  of growth leads, 46–47
  of organizational cultures
    on action taking, 52
    on communication, 50–51
    on decision-making, 52–53
    determining, 49–50
infrequent testing, 155
Innovation & Agility quadrant, 55
input time, 87
Intercom website, 211
internal data
  overview, 120
  user experience insights, 121
  user flow insights, 120
internally focused, 47
interviewing customer, 125–127

J

Jantsch, John, 62
Janz, Christoph, 214

job title, 22
Johns, Andy, 112

K

Kaushik, Avinash
  inventing HiPPO phrase, 132
  website by, 212
key business measurements, 76–77
key performance indicators (KPIs), 45

L

lagging indicator, 106
language fit, 82
leading indicator, 106
lean startup, growth hacking vs., 16–17
learning
  creating culture of, 26
  ignoring importance of, 202
  instilling culture of, 190
  from other growth lead, 175–176
  from tests
    inconclusive, 161–162
    overview, 157–163
    successful, 158–160
    systemizing changes, 162–163
    unsuccessful, 160–161

M

Mares, Justin, 83
marketing. *See also* advertising
  applying scientific method to, 21
  customer journey and, 82
  email marketing
    as part of channel expertise layer, 32
    as way to acquire users, 84
  engineering as
    as part of channel expertise layer, 32
    as way to acquire users, 84
  funnel marketing, 31
  goals of, 16

About the Author

Anuj Adhiya is the VP of Growth at Jamber (https://www.jamber.com/), the world's first Handware company committed to improving the quality of life of people by designing products made to be handheld. He is responsible for accelerating the adoption of the company's life-changing products among its target market. Additionally, he is a growth mentor at Seedstars and a marketing specialist at Harvard Innovation Labs. At both places, he coaches start-ups to help uncover their best growth opportunities and solve early growth challenges. Before this, he was the Category Growth Lead at The Predictive Index, where he owned the site responsible for successfully launching the talent optimization category. He was also the Director of Engagement and Analytics at GrowthHackers, where he grew the world's largest growth community working directly with Sean Ellis, the godfather of growth hacking.

Dedication

This book is dedicated to my parents. Their encouragement makes everything possible.

Author's Acknowledgments

I'd like to express my gratitude to everyone who has helped me write and produce this book. Firstly, I need to thank Anum Hussain, who put me in contact with Wiley. Her willingness to make the introduction set in place the chain of events that led to this book becoming a reality.

Secondly, if Sean Ellis wouldn't have taken a chance on a random person all those years ago, this book might not exist — and certainly not the way it's turned out. I've learned much in my growth journey from others, but none of that would have been possible without Sean giving me the that first shot.

I've had many people I consider to be unofficial mentors on the topic of growth. They may not even know this and may even take a minute to remember my name, but this is as good a time as any to explicitly recognize James Currier, Brian Balfour, and Andy Johns as having had immeasurable impact on the way I think about sustainable growth.

Similarly, there are many others who've played their part in opening my eyes to aspects of growth that I would never have considered. The biggest influences on me have had their sites listed in the final chapter of this book.

While I don't have the space to list the specific aspects they helped with, without the input of the following awesome growth professionals, this book would not be what it is: Luke Thomas, Satwik Govindarajula, Arpit Chaudhary, Andrew Capland, Andrew Miller, Lauralynn Stubler, Nelio Leone, Doug Odewahn-Oxley, Nanda Kumar, Dan Sullivan, Faisal Al-Khalidi, David Arnoux, Pedro Clivati, Shane Corstorphine, Nancy Hensley, Sebastian Almnes, Max van den Ingh, Gino Arendsz, Jordan Hwang, Julie Zhou, Guillaume Cabane, Lauren Schuman, Vivek Nanda, Hila Qu, Aaron Dun, Nadya Khoja, Andy Carvell, Maja Voje, Yara Paoli, Shanik Patel, and Sebastian Beja.

I can't even begin to express how helpful the support of my family during this process was. Being left alone to focus and write as and when I needed to be was a luxury without which there's no way I would have finished the book.

Lastly, I need to thank the supportive editorial team at Wiley for their monk-like patience with a first-time writer who gave them more than their fair share of heart attacks over whether this book would get published on time. So here's to Steve Hayes, Paul Levesque, Becky Whitney, and other editorial staff — there is literally no way this book would have gotten over the finish line without you.

Publisher's Acknowledgments

Acquisitions Editor: Steve Hayes

Senior Project Editor: Paul Levesque

Copy Editor: Becky Whitney

Editorial Assistant: Matthew Lowe

Sr. Editorial Assistant: Cherie Case

Production Editor: Siddique Shaik

Cover Image: @ Zketch/Shutterstock

Leverage the power

Dummies is the global leader in the reference category and one of the most trusted and highly regarded brands in the world. No longer just focused on books, customers now have access to the dummies content they need in the format they want. Together we'll craft a solution that engages your customers, stands out from the competition, and helps you meet your goals.

Advertising & Sponsorships

Connect with an engaged audience on a powerful multimedia site, and position your message alongside expert how-to content. Dummies.com is a one-stop shop for free, online information and know-how curated by a team of experts.

- Targeted ads
- Video
- Email Marketing
- Microsites
- Sweepstakes sponsorship

20 MILLION PAGE VIEWS EVERY SINGLE MONTH

15 MILLION UNIQUE VISITORS PER MONTH

43% OF ALL VISITORS ACCESS THE SITE VIA THEIR MOBILE DEVICES

700,000 NEWSLETTER SUBSCRIPTIONS TO THE INBOXES OF *300,000* UNIQUE INDIVIDUALS EVERY WEEK

# of dummies

Custom Publishing

Reach a global audience in any language by creating a solution that will differentiate you from competitors, amplify your message, and encourage customers to make a buying decision.

- Apps
- Books
- eBooks
- Video
- Audio
- Webinars

Brand Licensing & Content

Leverage the strength of the world's most popular reference brand to reach new audiences and channels of distribution.

For more information, visit **dummies.com/biz**

PERSONAL ENRICHMENT

Staying Sharp	Facebook	Guitar	Investing	Beekeeping	Digital Photography
9781119187790	9781119179030	9781119293354	9781119293347	9781119310068	9781119235606
USA $26.00	USA $21.99	USA $24.99	USA $22.99	USA $22.99	USA $24.99
CAN $31.99	CAN $25.99	CAN $29.99	CAN $27.99	CAN $27.99	CAN $29.99
UK £19.99	UK £16.99	UK £17.99	UK £16.99	UK £16.99	UK £17.99

Meditation	Pregnancy	Samsung Galaxy S7	iPhone	Crocheting	Nutrition
9781119251163	9781119235491	9781119279952	9781119283133	9781119287117	9781119130246
USA $24.99	USA $26.99	USA $24.99	USA $24.99	USA $24.99	USA $22.99
CAN $29.99	CAN $31.99	CAN $29.99	CAN $29.99	CAN $29.99	CAN $27.99
UK £17.99	UK £19.99	UK £17.99	UK £17.99	UK £16.99	UK £16.99

PROFESSIONAL DEVELOPMENT

 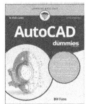     

Windows 10	AutoCAD	Excel 2016	QuickBooks 2017	macOS Sierra	LinkedIn	Windows 10
9781119311041	9781119255796	9781119293439	9781119281467	9781119280651	9781119251132	9781119310563
USA $24.99	USA $39.99	USA $26.99	USA $26.99	USA $29.99	USA $24.99	USA $34.00
CAN $29.99	CAN $47.99	CAN $31.99	CAN $31.99	CAN $35.99	CAN $29.99	CAN $41.99
UK £17.99	UK £27.99	UK £19.99	UK £19.99	UK £21.99	UK £17.99	UK £24.99

SharePoint 2016	Fundamental Analysis	Networking	Office 2016	Office 365	Salesforce.com	Coding
9781119181705	9781119263593	9781119257769	9781119293477	9781119265313	9781119239314	9781119293323
USA $29.99	USA $26.99	USA $29.99	USA $26.99	USA $24.99	USA $29.99	USA $29.99
CAN $35.99	CAN $31.99	CAN $35.99	CAN $31.99	CAN $29.99	CAN $35.99	CAN $35.99
UK £21.99	UK £19.99	UK £21.99	UK £19.99	UK £17.99	UK £21.99	UK £21.99

Learning Made Easy

ACADEMIC

9781119293576
USA $19.99
CAN $23.99
UK £15.99

9781119293637
USA $19.99
CAN $23.99
UK £15.99

9781119293491
USA $19.99
CAN $23.99
UK £15.99

9781119293460
USA $19.99
CAN $23.99
UK £15.99

9781119293590
USA $19.99
CAN $23.99
UK £15.99

9781119215844
USA $26.99
CAN $31.99
UK £19.99

9781119293378
USA $22.99
CAN $27.99
UK £16.99

9781119293521
USA $19.99
CAN $23.99
UK £15.99

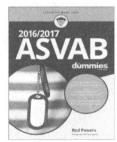

9781119239178
USA $18.99
CAN $22.99
UK £14.99

9781119263883
USA $26.99
CAN $31.99
UK £19.99

Available Everywhere Books Are Sold

Small books for big imaginations

9781119177173
USA $9.99
CAN $9.99
UK £8.99

9781119177272
USA $9.99
CAN $9.99
UK £8.99

9781119177241
USA $9.99
CAN $9.99
UK £8.99

9781119177210
USA $9.99
CAN $9.99
UK £8.99

9781119262657
USA $9.99
CAN $9.99
UK £6.99

9781119291336
USA $9.99
CAN $9.99
UK £6.99

9781119233527
USA $9.99
CAN $9.99
UK £6.99

9781119291220
USA $9.99
CAN $9.99
UK £6.99

9781119177302
USA $9.99
CAN $9.99
UK £8.99

Unleash Their Creativity

CPSIA information can be obtained
at www.ICGtesting.com
Printed in the USA
LVHW102040010420
651908LV00004B/40